Divine
Intervention

JOSEPH CAPPUCCI

ISBN 979-8-89428-998-4 (paperback)
ISBN 979-8-89526-000-5 (digital)

Copyright © 2024 by Joseph Cappucci

All rights reserved. No part of this publication may be reproduced, distributed, or transmitted in any form or by any means, including photocopying, recording, or other electronic or mechanical methods without the prior written permission of the publisher. For permission requests, solicit the publisher via the address below.

Christian Faith Publishing
832 Park Avenue
Meadville, PA 16335
www.christianfaithpublishing.com

All verses included in this book are from KJV.

Printed in the United States of America

This book is dedicated to my Lord and Savior, Jesus Christ. I am 100 percent certain that without Him, I would be destined for eternal confinement in hell after my death. As a sinner, I would have earned that fate and deserved nothing less. However, "God demonstrated His love toward us in that while we were yet sinners, Christ died for us" (Rom. 5:8). I only need to insert the words *me* and *I* in that magnificent verse instead of *us* and *we*. Now my eternal salvation and my eternal destiny are 100 percent secure and certain. I am sealed unto the day of redemption because of the finished work of Christ's vicarious sacrifice on the cross of Calvary (Eph. 4:30). "Therefore, if any man be in Christ he is a new creature. Old things are passed away, behold all things have become like new" (2 Cor. 5:17). I am eternally grateful to Jesus, my Savior. He has set me free and redeemed me from the bondage and penalty of sin. He has rescued me from the grip of Satan and taken the sting out of death. "Therefore there is now no more condemnation to those that are in Christ Jesus" (Rom. 8:1). "Neither is there salvation in any other: for there is none other name under Heaven given among men, whereby we must be saved" (Acts 4:12). The only response to these wonderful verses of Scripture is a hardy, hallelujah and amen!

Contents

Footsteps 1

Abduction 4

Poison Ivy...9

Town Beach 14

Dome Light 18

Angels in College...24

White River Vermont.....................................29

Marathon Bleed 35

Take Me Out to the Ball Game 44

An Old Friend..51

Hawaii Stones 57

Under the Trestle..69

Backpack Nomad 74

Wheelbarrow..83

Enough with the Leaves Already!........................95

My Marine Meets Hanna 106

A Daughter's Intuition 118

Ivy on the Beach..129

One Step One Second 136

My Personal Testimony of Salvation 142

The Gospel 156

Conclusion..167

Invitation 173

Footsteps

Where would my life be today without God's divine intervention? The answer, at least to me, is blatantly obvious. I would not be here. I would have died several times over! That begs another question: had I breathed my last breath, where would my eternal soul and spirit have finally resided? We will save the answer to that question for later.

The Almighty Creator is sovereign. He is the King of kings and the Lord of lords. The universe and everything in it belong to Him. He spoke everything that exists into existence. Even now, God sustains the entire universe in order to support life here on planet Earth. The very molecules of oxygen in your lungs are held together by our Creator! There is absolutely nothing that can occur on this blue-green terrestrial globe, suspended in the Milky Way Galaxy, without God's allowance. The Old Testament book of Job clearly bares out this truth. God is in complete and total control of each and every detail of the circumstances of our lives. All things are in His charge, and all things work together for good.

Could it be that God has already ordered our footsteps? Is our life's path already laid out before us? Is God steering our destiny to an expected end? Those are but three out of endless, deep theological questions. I dare say they are beyond the scope and breadth of my limited human understanding. I do believe, however, that everything God allows in a person's life here on earth will ultimately be used to bring about God's will for that person's life. At the end of the day, God's sovereign will will always be accomplished; it will ultimately bring glory, honor, and praise to His name. It is not my intention in this book to delve into deep systematic theologies like Arminianism (free will) or Calvinism (predestination). My goal is quite simply to shine a light on the numerous workings of the supernatural God—a God who is very much alive and involved and who even delights Himself in the daily affairs of His creation, more specifically us. He is the God who watches over, protects, and guides His creation. He is the God who "we love him because he first loved us" (1 Jn 1:19). He is the God whose ultimate desire is to "draw all men unto myself" (John 12:32).

The following collection of true experiences will give you but a mere glimpse of how the eternal God has supernaturally and divinely intervened in my path at various times in my life. At the same time, God has also, through divine intervention, put me in other people's paths as well. The end result was always the *Lord* accomplishing His perfect and divine will. To be used by God in some of these amazing instances as a vessel or perhaps an ambassador to the kingdom is humbling to the uttermost. I consider it to be the greatest calling and privilege of my life. To be called a servant to the King of kings and the Lord of lords is His gift to me. It is my highest honor and privilege to serve the one who died for me, who forgives me, and who rose from the dead and paid my sin debt in full. This King Jesus lives forevermore and shall one day return! Make no mistake about it! God is alive and well. Miracles are quite real! My greatest desire is that, as you read the following stories, you will see the Almighty hand of the one true living God, orchestrating all of the miraculous and minute details. My greatest hope is that you realize there is *no* such thing as a coincidence. Read attentively and open your heart so that you may see God for all that He is and all that He does. I pray earnestly that by seeing you believe and by believing, you trust in Him, and by trusting in Him, you call out to Him. Trust in Him alone for your daily provisions in this temporal, blink of an eye, life. Moreover, trust in Him for the deliverance of your soul and spirit to eternal and everlasting life in His kingdom, the kingdom of heaven. The Apostle Paul affirms, "But as it is written, eye hath not seen, nor ear heard, neither have entered into the heart of man, the things which God hath prepared for them that love Him" (1 Cor 2:9). It's going to be incredible!

Abduction

I grew up in the city of Somerville, Massachusetts. As a young boy between the ages of seven and ten, I used to ride my bicycle everywhere. The years were from 1969 to 1972. I would ride my bike to surrounding cities that were far past the street boundaries of our humble two-family residence 13 Thorndike Street. Unbeknownst to my parents, I was far from home, often into mischief, and where I should not have been. Of course, it was all in the spirit of an independent, adventurous, and curious city kid. It was a different day and age back then. Kids were allowed to go out and play in the summertime and be back home when the streetlights came on. All this freedom without your parents being a nervous wreck and worrying where you were.

Climbing to the tops of factory and store roofs and walking around up there was an everyday past time. Roaming in and out of parked train boxcars was the adventure of a lifetime. I can remember exploring, room by room and floor by floor, buildings that had recently been engulfed in flames and were

DIVINE INTERVENTION

boarded up and shut down. I would find a way in and make my way around a smoky-smelling, wet and black soot, charred, and burned-out building. These empty and abandoned remnants of factories or stores would become my personal treasure trove of youthful exploration. Many times throughout my adventures, I would come across homeless men attempting to shelter in these buildings and boxcars. Hobos, I would call them. I would find them sleeping in the bushes alongside the railroad train tracks as well. They would also be cozied up in parked buses at the depots I roamed around in. They were always nestled up to a *Playboy* or *Penthouse* magazine amid a bunch of newspapers that were used like blankets. Plenty of empty liquor bottles were always strewn about. On an unfortunate side note, it was probably not a very good thing to be exposed to graphic pornographic images from the books they left behind. At the tender age of seven or eight years old, those images would only serve to impact and scar my understanding and perception of women as I grew older.

During these adventures, my little friends and I used to go to this place called the screen yard. It was situated alongside the railroad tracks. The place was a junkyard comprised of piled-high wood, aluminum, and screen doors. We would climb in and out of the hiding places within all these doors and explore whatever needed exploring. You always had to be on the lookout for "the guy!" One day, while at the bottom of a cave made by many doors stacked up on top of each other, I heard those fateful words. Run, it's the guy! We scattered like rats climbing out of a sinking ship! I climbed up and out of the doors and ran to the back of the roof of the screen yard. I scooted myself over the edge of the roof and hung down with the railroad tracks about six feet below my feet. It was quite a jump, I might add. I was terrified, but I released my vice-grip fingers from the roof edge and then jumped! I jumped right into the strong grasp of a man who I now recall to be around sixty or more years old. He was a gruff-looking old man. Very stern comes to mind. I can still remember that he was unshaven with a rough and whiskered face. He smelled of booze, and he terrified me! This scary, mean-looking man grabbed me up as I hit the ground. He forcibly walked me and pulled me by my arm to a car on the back side of the railroad tracks. The man handled me more than my own father would ever even think of. He opened the passenger door, threw me inside, pushed the lock button down, and slammed the door closed. I sat there frozen, petrified! He then made his way around the back of the car and headed toward the driver's door. That's when *it* happened!

As I sat paralyzed in the front passenger seat of the car, I had a strange sense. A feeling came over me. It was as if time had stopped and I was in slow motion. Let's recall that at this time, I was seven or eight years old. I remember that my mind was extremely focused and trained on one thing. It was as though I was in a dream state. *Joseph, get out of the car!* The voice in my head was beyond clear. The timing had to be perfect, though, lest I be overtaken and snatched up. I sat still

DIVINE INTERVENTION

and let my eyes rove to the right side as if you were looking over your shoulder. I did not move my head even an inch. I was motionless except for my eyes. It was as though they became like eyes in the back of my head. My mind, or what I would call the voice in my head, made me keenly aware of the fact that I had to wait to make my move. *Wait! Wait! Stay calm, Joseph. Wait till he is all the way around the back of the car and ready to open his door on the driver's side. Then make your move when he is the furthest from you.*

Furthest from you—it was so powerful that I can still hear that instruction echoing in my mind like it was yesterday. The details of the escape were embedded in my mind and were exquisite. They still resonate with me to this day. It was perfectly clear to me that I was to wait for the exact moment his hand reached for the driver's door handle. I sat very still, not moving a muscle. I was sitting very quietly, all alone in this nightmare. It was as if I were being obedient and fully accepting of my demise. Except for the darting of my eyes, first to the right as he walked away from the passenger door and then to the left as he approached the driver's door, I sat as still as a frightened mouse. As my abductor was mumbling words I couldn't quite make out, he reached for his door handle. At that precise second, I pulled up the lock button, grabbed the handle, and flung my door open. I ran down the railroad tracks as fast as my little legs could carry me. Looking back at my captor was not even an option. I never looked back, not once, until I made it to the steps of my front porch. The relief I felt was overwhelming. I caught my breath and was overjoyed that I was safe. Even at the young age of seven or eight, I remember having a thankful heart for God for making it home safely. I never told my parents of this ordeal till years later in my adulthood.

What I realize today is that God was sitting with me in the front seat of that car on that day many years ago. He was there the entire time. I was not all alone, as I once thought. His Spirit was whispering in my ear the entire time. He was making it very clear to me everything that I had to do. He kept me focused on the task at hand with a certain calm. Forty-six years later, I now know that God preserved my life that day and kept my photograph from ending up on a milk carton as a missing child. I know in my heart of hearts that the stern and scary drunkard man had no good intentions for me. I felt his evil as he roughly pulled me toward his car and threw me in the front seat. I don't want to even imagine the possible outcomes had I not escaped. God divinely intervened in my life and made His presence known to me. He shrouded me in His protection. He calmed my spirit and gave me the plan, the ability, and the courage to follow through. He saved my life that day. There is no way that escape strategy came to a little seven- or eight-year-old boy. I did not come up with that plan or the courage I needed all on my own. There would be countless more times God would intervene on my behalf, protecting and preserving my life. In particular for a day that would come many years down the road.

Poison Ivy

At the age of ten, my parents fulfilled a dream in my life. They moved our family from the big city of Somerville, Massachusetts, to the rural country. We then called Groton, Massachusetts, our new hometown. It was a beautiful little town about thirty-five miles northwest of Somerville. Living in the country can come with some different hazards than in the city. These hazards came in the form of poisonous plants that, if exposed to, could wreak havoc on your life. At thirteen years old, I was selected to play for the all-star team in my town's major league baseball game. I was in seventh grade, and it was a great way to be recognized by all your friends. Actually, it was a great way to get the cute girls to take notice too. As game day approached, I began to run into a very itchy problem. The worst case of poison ivy I had ever experienced engulfed both my feet. The liquid-filled blisters covered the entire bottoms of both feet and all between my toes. Surely I could not let this ridiculous rash get in the way of the limelight of playing and actually pitching in that all-star game.

The bubbles grew in size; they were huge and filled with liquid. There was no way I could get a sock on, let alone a baseball cleat. I decided to take matters into my own hands, or should I say feet? I played doctor, popped all the blisters with a sewing pin, and peeled the skin off. I then proceeded to plunge my feet into every concoction known to mankind. At first, it was pure bleach with a little warm water. Next, I moved on to iodine and Mercurochrome. You may remember that Mercurochrome was a topical antiseptic containing mercury. It came in a small bottle with a little stick dispenser. I would dip the stick in the red liquid and then roll it over the open, raw blister wounds on the bottom of my feet. Calamine lotion and Caladryl lotion were my next cures du jour. Various different poison ivy creams and sprays were applied at heavy rates as well. Last but not least, I soaked my feet in straight isopropyl rubbing alcohol. Nothing was going to stand in the way of me taking the mound on an all-star game day! I was determined to keep those blisters at bay and prevent them from ever returning.

I played in the all-star game, and my team won. Not many days later, I was having difficulty walking. It seemed like my groin was very stiff on both sides of the upper inside of my legs. I had resorted to using crutches to get around because of how sore my feet and groin were. I was also experiencing nausea and extreme weakness, and I was lightheaded. I remember being in the garage and getting an odor of exhaust from a car running in the driveway. Unfortunately,

DIVINE INTERVENTION

that was all that was needed for me to pass out on the garage floor. My foster brother, Mickey, picked me up and carried me to my bed. At some point later in the day, my dad was walking by my room and noticed me in my bed. He told to me to get up and eat. He suggested to get some fresh air outside. He said I had fainted because I needed to eat something and was weak. I was very confused by his suggestions, and I had no idea what meal I was supposed to eat. I also had no idea what time of day it was or even which day it was. I clearly remember the sun coming through the window, not knowing if it was morning, noon, or sundown. I was in real trouble! You have to remember that back in the day, parents didn't run to the hospital for every little thing. Not to sound crass or rude, but there was a little ignorance involved. My mom was somewhat concerned about my symptoms and decided to give the local emergency room a call and ask some questions. Upon the hospital's suggestion, my parents took me in straight away.

The emergency room physicians attended to me immediately! I will never forget the look on the doctor's face as he inspected my feet and the massive infection that was overtaking my body. I clearly recall the ER doctor telling my mom that I may not have made it through the night if they hadn't brought me in. He had mentioned that if I were left home to sleep that night, the morning may have found me in a coma, if not dead. I had massive blood poisoning! My white blood cell count was three to four times the normal limit. The number was off the charts.

There were red infection lines starting at the bottom of my feet, tracking up both legs, and into the lymph nodes in both my left and right groin. The lymph nodes were full of poison. That's why my legs were stiff. The lines continued up past my groin and into my abdominal area. All the chemical cocktails I had been immersing my feet in in order to play America's favorite pastime were killing me. Massive antibiotics and a week in the hospital with a hoop or arc at the end of my bed brought healing and recovery. The hoop was put in place so the sheet and blanket didn't touch my wounds. By the way, it's important to note that my mom and dad had no idea I was playing doctor behind the closed doors of the bathroom with all my foot-healing potions.

Once again, my time to depart the planet had not yet arrived. My dad, innocently enough, thought that perhaps some food and fresh air would do the trick. My mom wasn't entirely aware that there was any big problem at all. My parents just weren't aware of how sick I really was or how grave the situation had become. God allowed me to wake up from fainting and approach my mom with my ill-feeling complaints. At this stage, I believe God used His Spirit to move my mom. He prompted her to make a phone call—a call, which in turn resulted in saving my life. He supernaturally inspired her to pick up the phone receiver and make a query. God, in His mercy, did not allow the poison to take my life. The poison was only inches from reaching my heart! He halted it in time for me to be saved. God was actively at work in

DIVINE INTERVENTION

the details of what was happening in my thirteenth year of life that summer of 1975. God is the giver and taker of life. No one will endure any situation or live or die through any circumstance without the express allowance of the Almighty. No person will depart from this planet earth without the sovereign God of the universe determining the place and time. As I relate more of my life's experiences throughout the pages to follow, you will begin to see that fact become more and more evident. Coincidences cease appearing to be coincidences!

Town Beach

One of the many wonderful amenities of living in the country is swimming at the local lake. In Groton, it was Knops Pond. Every day of the summer, I would do my prescribed chores. Mowing the lawn and raking up the grass shavings were among the top two chores on my dad's to-do list. Once the chores were completed to dad's satisfaction, it was off to the town beach, hopefully. "Can I go now, Dad?" His answer was always the same: "Now you can go." Yay! I would hop on my bike, throw a towel around my neck, and pedal my way two miles down the road to the beach.

This particular summer was a hot and humid one. The beach was always packed during the week, mostly with moms and their young kids. The beach had a T-shaped dock with multiple ladders affixed to it in order to get back up on the dock. All of us teenagers had so much fun jumping off and swimming back to it. A lot of time was spent just standing on the dock, soaking up the sun, and catching up with friends about how their summer was going. Of course, there was always time to flirt with all the girls as well. There was only one lifeguard on duty. He or she had the job of watching around fifty to sixty swimmers at any given time. They certainly had their work cut out for them.

On one particular sunny day, there were a lot of little kids in the water. The lifeguard appeared to be tanned, calm, and in control of things. I happened to be standing on the dock, chatting it up with some friends. Inadvertently, while chatting it up with friends, I looked down in the water to the inside right of the T dock and noticed something out of place. Something just didn't seem right. I just kept looking at what appeared to be a little child's head just below the surface of the water. The child's little arms were flailing in a frenzied attempt to reach the side of the dock. However, the kid wasn't going anywhere fast, and the dock was well out of reach. I still wasn't sure what I was seeing. The place was packed with little kids! Maybe I was a little in shock or disbelief. Believe it or not, I was stuck in watch mode, not really realizing what was potentially happening. I had to make sure I wasn't seeing things. Finally, my slow, fifteen-year-old teenage brain kicked in and figured it out. I jumped into neck-deep water and waded a couple of steps toward this little kid. I proceeded to reach my hands under the armpits of this child and quickly lifted a beautiful little girl out of the water. Her face was blue, and she was gasping for breath. She was in a terrified state. I believe she may have known just how close she had come to her demise. There is no doubt.

She was well on her way to drowning. I continued to hold this precious little girl, who appeared to be four or five years old, in my arms and walked out of the water, headed toward the beach.

The lifeguard was clueless about any of this drama that was being played out. Literally clueless! I remember walking right past him with the little girl in my arms while he sat on his stand. For him, it was just another day at the beach, no pun intended. I asked the child to help me find her mommy. The little girl was able to show me where her mom and their blanket were. At that point, I handed off the crying child to her mom. The mom took her little girl from my arms and thanked me. It was strange. I expected the mother to be jumping for joy with wild elation over the return of her nearly drowned child to safety. What I remember was a much less enthusiastic response. I must admit, I was somewhat stunned. Perhaps the mom was in shock, disbelief, or a little embarrassed by the whole ordeal. I know this: she had no idea where her daughter was or the life-threatening dilemma she was facing. What's more important, though, is that a certain tragedy was avoided. A beautiful little girl was rescued and able to go on with her life.

So the theme continues. Divine intervention at the lake! I was in the designated spot that God had placed me on that summer day long ago. Right where I was supposed to be and at the exact appointed time. A minute longer mowing the lawn, raking the grass shavings, or chatting with my dad would have meant

DIVINE INTERVENTION

the difference between life and death for the beautiful little brown-haired girl. The girl had huge wide blue eyes and countless freckles. Yes, I remember every detail of her face. A precious, cute little face that I will never forget. Her little pouting countenance is embedded in my memory. She glared right into my eyes when I lifted her out of the water as she gasped for air. She held me so tight, as if I were a family member. She was absolutely aware of the fact that she had been rescued. I knew in that moment that I had saved her life. Ironically, I never got this little girl's name.

Was it a coincidence, or did God direct my eyes and my attention to that specific area of water at the T dock? No one has to convince me that the Almighty God had a different plan for that little girl on that hot summer day. I can only imagine what footsteps God has ordered for the rest of her life. He allowed her to live and once again orchestrated every detail of the fateful day at the lake. I know I was used by God—used for His will in her life. Of course, I don't mean used in a bad sense of the word. A better rendition might be that I was a vessel, a willing servant. It is so humbling! What a blessing! Why me? Perhaps this little girl became an educator, a doctor, or a water safety instructor. Maybe a swim coach or even a lifeguard! Maybe a Christian. Perhaps one day there will be a reunion. Only then will I know for sure what became of her life. This time, I'll be sure to ask her name. To God be the glory, great thing He has done!

Dome Light

I regret to say that my high school years were "a little" on the wild side. Bonfires and beers were a favorite pastime. Overindulging and staying out too late were far too much the norm rather than the exception. I don't want to glorify my deeds back then, but suffice to say that life was a little on the wild side. I certainly sowed my share of wild oats.

Roughly about age seventeen, my friends and I were at a local party. We were partaking in liquid refreshments and engaging in fine conversation with our female counterparts. As the night grew late and the party drew to a close, it was time to head home. Often, I would be the one to drive at least three or four of us home. I am ashamed to say that, in most cases, I was not fully sober. At the same time, I did not trust anybody else driving me home after a night of drinking alcohol and partying. I always figured I was more sober than the rest and too controlling to let anyone else drive. Each and every time before driving, I would conduct an inventory of my condition. A self-examination as to whether I was able to

DIVINE INTERVENTION

get me and my friend's home safe. It's not my intent to justify drinking and driving at all. In fact, it was careless, stupid, and illegal. When I got behind the wheel, however, it was all business, and my only focus was taking care of my passengers and getting everybody home safely to bed. I guess you could say I straightened up real fast when it came time to be the shuttle driver. Often, there were times I actually walked my pals to their doors in the early hours of the morning. If I was not able to drive, I would call my mom and inform her that sleeping over was the best option. She never argued with me and understood my reason for staying out. When I did come home, I would always stop by her bedroom, sit on the side of the bed, and watch a little TV with her. She stayed up late most nights, watching a portable TV on her nightstand. This is how she would nod off.

This one particular night after the party, I was driving three friends' homes. I seem to recall it was around 1:30 a.m. We were on our town's main road, Route 119, a.k.a. Boston Road. We were headed west toward the center of town, toward my friend's house. My passengers were all in the process of passing out. They would wake up upon arrival at their homes when I called them to get up. Suddenly, my attention was drawn to a very faint light off in the woods on the other side of the road. It was about twenty or thirty yards into the woods. I just sped by it, going about forty-five to fifty miles per hour. However, something didn't add up. An uncanny sense overcame me. That light had no business being there. I had driven by that same spot countless times on the school bus and in cars. I knew there was nothing at that spot in those woods. So I informed my friends of my concern. Their response was that I was crazy, had too many beers, and "Take us home!" They clearly were not seeing what I was. I turned the car around and headed east again to pass the spot and get a better look. This time, I was on the same side of the road as the light and was closer to it. I went past it, looked hard, and turned around again, heading west toward town, much to the complaints of my pals. They still didn't get it. Their only thought was of collapsing in their beds. Also, at this point, I think they were starting to get carsick. My brain would not let this go. Something was amiss. Finally, I turned around and headed back to that side of the road where the dim light was on. I parked the car on the shoulder of the road and stared extremely hard into those woods, noticing the dim light off in the distance. At this juncture, my friends thought I was a drunken fool!

I exited my car and walked up an embankment with one friend lagging far behind me. I started into the woods and toward the light. In a matter of seconds, the situation became very apparent to me. Oh my gosh! A car was in the woods, covered with dirt, sticks, pine needles, leaves, and everything else. The mystery light was a dimly lit dome light that was on. It was very faintly lit. The hood was bent up, and the windshield glass was cracked. I hurried to the driver's side of the car to find a woman badly hurt with the steering wheel crushing her abdomen. I yelled to my

DIVINE INTERVENTION

friends to get help! This was around the years 1980 to 1981—well, before the cell phone invention. I had been wearing a sporty Members Only jacket that evening. So I took it off and covered her torso, but not before I bent the steering wheel up and off her stomach. It took some brute strength as the steering wheel was nearly bent in half. Her face was bloody and swollen; she was definitely in shock, and she was coming in and out of consciousness. Her age was probably twenty-five to thirty years old. She kept calling me Al. "Please help me, Al," was her repeated mantra. I assured her that she was going to be okay, that I would stay with her, and that help was on the way.

This woman ended up in the woods when her car failed to make a right-hand turn and stayed straight. It went up a little embankment where it went airborne, passing through two pine trees on either side, slamming to rest at the base of another pine tree. The car looked as though it were camouflaged from all the debris that settled on it.

After covering her with my jacket, bending the steering wheel off her abdomen, and trying to soothe her, I went for help. I wasn't exactly sure if my buddies were successful in getting help, so I had to make sure. The nearest house was approximately thirty to forty yards away. Clearly, in that moment, I was probably experiencing a bit of shock myself. I began pounding on a stranger's door. At this point, it has to be nearing 2:00 a.m. I was somewhat becoming frantic, surmising that perhaps this woman may be fatally injured! A Japanese man with his wife came to the door in his robe. I was frantically telling him, in a panic, of the ordeal transpiring and to please let me use the phone to call for help. He was very shaken up; I suspect even scared, to say the least, as this young high school kid reeking of alcohol had just barged into his house running to his phone. I acted as if the house were my own. Admittedly, I was in shock and a little under the influence. When I think back on my arrogance in entering that man's home with his wife present at such an insane hour, I can only feel shame. I could discern that the home owner was very shaken up by my intrusion. I justified my actions at the time due to the calamity at hand and for the greater good. The proper call was made, and before long, the EMTs, firemen, and police were on their way. I went back to the woman and stayed with her till they arrived on the scene. As they began to do their job of saving that woman, I made my way back to my car and drove off. I wasn't interested in hanging around with alcohol on my breath and being the driver! As was usual, my friends all arrived home safely that night, and so did I.

Really! What made me see that faint dome light? It was 1:30 a.m. I was driving forty-five to fifty miles per hour past it on the opposite side of the road. I was under the influence of alcohol. The light was faint at best and twenty to thirty yards away in the woods. I was consumed with determining the source and kept turning around and around like a mouse in a maze. It was a beacon that led me to another human being in a life-and-death situation. God never ceases to amaze me! When He determines to get something done, it gets done! The Almighty God of heaven and earth directed my footsteps that early morning. He alone brought that dome light to my attention. He directed my actions and motivated me to do His bidding. The sovereign God of the universe had determined that it was not checkout time for the lady in the car. Her life would continue. He can use any means at His disposal to accomplish His will for a person's life. That night, He used me despite the error of my foolish, teenage ways. He used the foolishness of a car dome light to compel me to see. I never caught that woman's name. Honestly, I never found out the outcome of her health either. I trust God had a purpose for me seeing that small dome light in the world that early morning. Maybe, one day, she and I will reunite and see the real light—the light of the world!

Angels in College

Oh, the college years! It was a time of independence, no parents, lots of beer, and unlimited freedom! Oh yeah, I almost forgot: continued education, maturation, and doing your own laundry! I went to North Adams State College in the Berkshires of Massachusetts. It was a beautiful campus nestled in the mountains in the northwest corner of Massachusetts. The Vermont and New York borders were minutes away. Mt. Greylock was the highest point in the state and was just ten minutes down the road from campus. My college buddies and I drove up and down that mountain on many occasions. The views were spectacular, and it was a great getaway excursion from the routine of class, studying, and tests. My major was business administration, and my concentration was management with a minor in Spanish. Those college days were some of the best and most memorable times of my life. They were also some of the most reckless and senseless times. By God's grace, I managed to survive this era of my life.

DIVINE INTERVENTION

It seemed like I was always in some sort of scuffle. Sometimes I think there is a price on my head. I had a reputation that preceded me. There can be no doubt it carried over from high school. Someone was always gunning for me—looking to knock my block off, instigate a fisticuff, and try to humble me. Needless to say, my fists had their work cut out for them. Defending myself was the norm, not the exception. When I look back on those days, one thought comes to mind: my juvenile behavior was most regrettable and downright stupid!

I happened to be at an off-campus party one night, where, as usual, the booze was flowing and much imbibing was to be had. My college buddy Glenn and I were just hanging out at this off-campus keg party, socializing. We were approached by some other students regarding "a situation." They informed us that a couple of guys, who were not students, but rather "townies," were inciting trouble with people at the party. Well, far be it for Glenn and me not to be the college social police. In fact, we were both members of the North Adams State College boxing club. We were under the false impression that it was our job to enforce the rule of law throughout the campus. We were no less than young punks with massive egos.

Glenn and I were told these guys exited the party and were headed across campus. The next thing you know, the hunt is on. We were highly motivated and highly intoxicated. We were also as angry as a couple of caged lions. We began a hot pursuit of these

JOSEPH CAPPUCCI

two troublemaking townies. Did I mention that the townies were the local indigenous people who had no business being on our campus? At least, that's how we perceived it in our little pea brains. Anyway, we were running at full speed in their direction. Then we started to see them up ahead; they were about fifty yards directly in front of us. Glenn and I were then 100 percent committed to having a full-blown confrontation with our local intruders. We were stripping off our shirts in a full-out sprint through the dark night. Bare chested now and all pumped up, we were about to put on a boxing clinic and box these guys around to our way of thinking. We needed to make an impression on them about not coming around the school anymore and causing trouble.

We had these guys in our sights and were ready to pounce, like the young lions we are. Our adrenalin was off the charts. Our brains were on overdrive and in kill mode. All of a sudden, with about twenty-five yards to go, something really strange ensued. Literally, out of the shadows, two college kids jumped right directly in our path. We never saw them until the last possible second. We had to stop very abruptly, lest they be bowled over by our forward momentum. Neither of us recognized these two kids, and we knew everybody on campus! It was a very small campus with only about two thousand students. We had no idea where they came from or how they just appeared out of the darkness to our right. They were holding us back from pursuing our prey. They actually had their hands on us to restrain us from going any fur-

DIVINE INTERVENTION

ther. They pleaded with us to give it up and head back to the party. They called us by our nicknames, Pooch and Decker. That was really odd, given we didn't know them. We were enraged at this point and didn't understand this untimely intercession or why it was a big concern. We were ready to overtake our prey, and now we were contemplating changing our mission to overtake these two peacemakers.

These two strangers, again, of whom we had no idea of their identity, told us that these townies were carrying guns. They told us that while at the off-campus house party, they flashed their handguns at some of the students and were really scary individuals. They assured us that they, too, had witnessed the townies brandishing the weapons themselves. We were never told this information as we began the chase. These two strangers who stepped out of the shadows insisted that this pursuit was not in our best interests. So with less than twenty-five yards to go and confronting these guys, Glenn and I looked at each other and instantly, without any hesitation, gave up chase and headed back to the party. The conviction in our minds to relent in this chase was overwhelming. Our pride was nowhere to be found. It didn't take any convincing whatsoever. There was no debate. As soon as the word *gun* was mentioned, it had a paralyzing and sobering effect. All of a sudden, we weighed everything in the balance. We both immediately realized that we had been rescued from something bigger than we were—something that could have meant the end of our young lives. We never even said thanks or bye to these mysterious fellas. Decker and I never did figure out who it was that stopped us dead in our tracks that night. Better yet, I should say, it stopped us alive in our tracks before we wound up dead. We never saw them again throughout the rest of our college days. Whoever they were, they never approached us again.

Thirty-four years later, I had my suspicions as to the events that occurred that dark night at North Adams State College. Those shadowy strangers saved our lives! We were certainly not angels in college, but that night, many years ago, there were angels among us. They were dispatched to our rescue. They were instructed to intervene. They were our guardians. I am reminded of the verse in the book of Hebrews: "Be not forgetful to entertain strangers: for thereby some have entertained angels unawares" (Heb. 13.2). At the time, I was unaware of the identity of our two guests from the shadows, but now, I am convinced, I know who they were. When I think back at how it all played out that night, I marvel and am humbled. Even though God was the furthest thought from my rebellious, self-absorbed, and arrogant mind, I wasn't far from God's loving and merciful mind. Once again, my life had been miraculously preserved. But for the grace of God, there go I. Please, God, keep on keeping on with your divine interventions. Don't let me ever stand in your way.

White River Vermont

graduated from college in 1985 with a bachelor of science degree in business administration. My wife and I were married in October 1988, and before too long, we were expecting our first child in December 1989. So much for not having kids until four or five years into the marriage. At the same time, I was self-employed, running my own life insurance agency. So with everything on my plate, it was time for the second annual road trip to Vermont with my old high school pals. I organized all the details of the trip, starting with making the reservations, going shopping for the food, and collecting the money from the guys. So in early May of 1989, with tents packed and sleeping bags loaded, the seven of us set out for the two-hour drive north to the White River camping area. It was situated in a little town in southern Vermont called Gaysville. Let the second annual White River, Vermont, camping trip begin.

The seven of us were very close in high school. It had been eight years since we graduated. We were all very excited and looking forward to bringing each other up to speed on the details of our lives since our last camping blast. It was a great camping spot, directly on the White River. The river rushed just a few yards in front of our tents. It was soothing to listen to and even better to fall asleep to, or, should I say, pass out to. At that time of the year, in early spring, the water was moving at a fast pace, and the water level was very high. This could be attributed to the snowmelt from the higher elevations and the spring rains. I remember the river current being very strong. The few times I waded in a couple of yards, I had to hold my ground or I would have been knocked over.

In the evenings, we did a lot of reminiscing around the campfire. There were many laughs to be had. We also drank a lot of alcohol, both beer and liquor. I will not lie; there was ample marijuana consumption as well. This partying carried on all day and all night. The pace was dizzying, literally. We played cards for money, we had whiffle ball games on the riverbank, and we sure played our fair share of drinking games. It was anarchy! When you put a bunch of twenty-something-year-olds together who were best buds in high school, there is bound to be some excitement and some potential trouble too.

Just outside the campground, there was a bridge that crossed the White River. Just ahead of the bridge, on the same side of the river as the campground, was a rock cliff. The cliff wall rose up about thirty-five feet above the brisk, moving river. For the second year in a row, my pals and I walked out of the campground and headed for the cliff. The year before, we

DIVINE INTERVENTION

had done the exact same excursion, and we were all jumping off the cliff wall into the river. It was great fun! We would jump and swim, then climb back up and jump again. This year, however, something was very different—very different and very dangerous!

As I ventured out onto the cliff and toward the edge, I was hyperaware. It probably had to do with the fact that I was under the influence of pot and was overanalyzing all the details. There was also alcohol in my bloodstream left over from the campfire shenanigans during the late night before. Of course, there was a fresh batch of alcohol coursing through my veins from drinking from the moment we woke up. I think the term we used to justify that behavior was "hair of the dog." I'm not so sure this was a camping trip meant for getting away to relax as much as it was about pushing all the limits and acting like senseless high school kids again.

So in this drunken and altered state, I paused at the edge of the cliff and began surveying the potential hazards of what I was about to do. All I could see and relate to was how fast the water was rushing by. I could also see whirlpools everywhere below the cliff. It was early May, and the water was dangerous! From my vantage point, I let the guys know that there would be no jumping off this year. The response was overwhelming. Comments like chicken and pussy were the put-downs du jour. My pals wanted me to jump regardless of the dangerous conditions. I insisted that it was way too perilous and wasn't going to jump! After that, my buddies unleashed a second wave of colorful put-downs worse than the first. I thought peer pressure disappeared after high school. Apparently not; anyway, I was weak and caved in like a new freshman looking to impress everyone.

I stepped a few feet back from the edge and began rationalizing in my mind. I was a lifeguard at a military base for two summers during college. I was also a strong swimmer, having taken advanced swimming and conditioning in college. I had to swim a timed mile to pass that swim course. Lastly, I was a strong athlete and surely could manage the swim back to the cliff wall and up the rocks. I'll show these guys! I had my sneakers on, a T-shirt, and shorts. My last comments to my friends were, "If anything happens to me, there is a sandbar over there, and that's where my body will likely end up. Please get to me quickly and give me CPR." How insane and completely reckless! What a foolish and juvenile mindset! My wife was two months pregnant with our first child! I was actually joking about life and death. Gosh! What a dope—no pun intended!

I ran as fast as possible and leaped out as far as I could. The entire way down, I was yelling very loud. Besides giving me a boost of adrenaline, the screaming served to expel any last breath left in me before entering the river. I entered the raging, ice-cold, freezing water. If yelling on the way down wasted what air I had remaining in my lungs, then the ice-cold water surely took away any last reserve of that precious oxygen. I went deep into the river, probably about eight to ten feet below the surface.

DIVINE INTERVENTION

I fully expected to have the current move me down the river. I never considered the fact that there was also a current that was pulling me down from below and holding me under the water. I kicked and pulled toward the surface with every ounce of power and strength I had within me. It was futile. I could see the surface a few feet above me, but I couldn't gain an inch. The current was like a pair of hands gripping my ankles and pulling me down. There was no time to see my life flash before my eyes. I was dying, and that was that. Terror was all that I knew in that moment. My life was over. My first and yet-to-be born son would be fatherless.

In the next moment, only my nostrils and mouth were barely breaking the surface of the freezing, raging water. It almost seemed as though I went through some sort of time warp. The last thing I was fully aware of was that I could not regain the surface, and death was certain. Suddenly, the safety of the cliff wall was directly about ten feet in front of me. With my mouth barely breaking the water's surface, I managed to kick my way to the rocks at the bottom of the cliff and pull my exhausted body up and out of the river and onto a rock. I held on for dear life as my breath returned to me. As I lied there, catching my breath, I was overwhelmed by thoughts of how crazy and stupid I was for jumping into the river. What was I thinking! I almost widowed my wife and abandoned my unborn child. I was also overwhelmed by a feeling of immense joy that I was alive and well.

What just happened? How did I get out? Did this really just happen? I should have drowned.

Only God and I know exactly what went down that early spring day on the White River in Vermont. Nobody else will ever understand what I experienced that day. My explanation doesn't do justice to what I felt. The words are hard to come by that could accurately describe the terror that gripped me from below the surface of that ice-cold river.

Mercy and love are two words that come to mind when I ponder the events that unfurled on that fateful morning. I am 100 percent convinced beyond a shadow of a doubt that God spared my stupid, drunken, and stoned life that day on the White River in a little town called Gaysville, Vermont. In early May of 1989, God dispatched an angel, or perhaps angels, to unleash the grip of death, which held my ankles and was pulling me under. I was slipping away in a watery grave. Not only was death's grip let loose, but the angels pushed me up those last four feet to the water's surface. They nudged me over to the rocks. They saved my life! I know that in heaven, if I were allowed to see the times in my life when God intervened, this near-drowning will surely be on the reel to reel. Oh, God, thank You! Thank You for watching over me when I was not watching over myself. Thank You, God, for reaching down into my life's timeline. Thank You, heavenly Father, for allowing me to be around and welcome my first son Adam into the world seven months later, in December 1989.

Marathon Bleed

Running has always been a passion in my life. I have been running since the good ole days of playing soccer in high school. I have also run countless five-mile and 10K road races over the years. The running addiction is real. It keeps you coming back because of the "runner's high" you experience. As you run, the body releases endorphins, which can give you a euphoric-like feeling. This addiction eventually led me to run further and longer. Half-marathons were next, and then onto some fifteen-mile. By now, you can probably guess where this is going. Once you reach those kinds of distances, you have no choice but to go for the pinnacle of road races. I was not going to stop until I had a marathon on my running résumé. Twenty-six miles and three hundred twenty-five yards was the new high bar to be achieved. I trained like never before and ended up running the 1990 Boston Marathon at the young age of twenty-seven years old. My best friend, Randy, and I ran together on that beautiful April day.

JOSEPH CAPPUCCI

I was doing great until about mile eighteen. At this mile marker of a marathon, your body has been depleted of a substance called glycogen. It's the sugar that fuels the muscles and maintains your work effort. Other chemicals, such as salt and potassium, have also been depleted. It all adds up to a running term known as "hitting the wall." This condition makes it very hard to endure the last few miles of any marathon and finish with your dignity still intact. The good news is that I did finish the Boston Marathon on sheer willpower in just under five hours. I was happy to finish, but unhappy with the time it took and the excruciating pain involved in those last few miles. I was hoping to run the marathon between four and four and a half hours. During the last six miles of that marathon route, a war was being waged between my mind and body just to get to the finish line. The war waged on, and I managed to cross that yellow finish line in front of the Boston Public Library. I'm not going to lie; I barely made it. Clearly, there was more and far better training to do for the next one.

After resting up for a couple of months and relaxing my race schedule, I decided that I had to try it again. So with a disappointing marathon time now behind me, I set out to conquer the 1991 Boston Marathon. My goal was to set a new personal record. I trained harder than the year before and was determined to crush my previous 1990 marathon time. When you run the kind of training schedule required to finish a marathon, you often encounter various

DIVINE INTERVENTION

injuries and maladies. Sore muscles are par for the course and can account for most of your problems. I happened to get a lot of pain in my lower legs up and down along the side of my calve muscles. Especially after my long runs, the pain would be the most prevalent. The pain made it very difficult to maintain my running schedule and to keep up with the miles I needed to log in order to be successful at finishing Boston. My solution to the leg pain came in the form of aspirin—Excedrin Extra Strength, to be exact. Why not? Wasn't aspirin a panacea? At least, that's what I thought.

I was at a point in my training schedule that ran five to six days a week. My runs would take me anywhere from a minimum of three miles upward to eighteen miles. Usually, I ran on a completely empty stomach except for two Excedrin Extra Strength to keep my lower leg pain at bay. The Excedrin was working quite well and allowed me to persevere in my running schedule. This regimen went on for about eight to ten weeks. Excedrin Extra Strength had become a daily staple in my diet.

Lo and behold, at around the ten-week mark, I started to feel lousy. I thought I had a stomach bug. I can remember having pain in my belly and also feeling dizzy and lightheaded. In addition, I also experienced shortness of breath and was winded easily. At one point, I recall walking from my car up to the post office entrance door and having to stop and catch my breath. *How can this be?* I pondered. *I just ran eighteen miles yesterday!* I had very bad diarrhea for a couple of days and assumed it was all part of this stomach flu. Oh, did I forget to mention that the diarrhea was completely black as tar and constant? Sorry about the graphic details! Against my stubborn will, I had to suspend my running schedule for a few days. I was too weak and sick to continue my runs.

After three or four days without a run, I began to go stir crazy. I felt as though the success of finishing the Boston Marathon was being sabotaged. I determined it was time to lace up the sneakers and hit the pavement again, ready or not. One of the lousy things about training in Boston is that you have to run throughout the cold New England winter. The race is in April. There is no way around it unless you run entirely indoors—boring! The weather conditions can be brutal! One cold January evening, I decided it was time to ignore this so-called stomach flu and press on through a quick five-mile. If I could work up a good sweat, then perhaps I could rid myself of whatever was ailing me. At least, that's what I told myself. I stood at my back door, all prepared for the freezing cold outside. I had my gloves on and a full-faced hat with a rubber face mask. As usual, I wore two or three layers of shirts with my Gore-Tex pants and jacket. Gore-Tex is great at keeping water off you while staying warm. The last thing I put on was my yellow nighttime reflector vest. Safety is of the utmost importance, especially while running in the black, cold New England winter nights.

I stood with my hand on the doorknob and a fresh new excitement about getting this workout done

DIVINE INTERVENTION

and perhaps feeling better. My wife was standing in the kitchen, facing me at the back door. Suddenly, my wife chimes in about me holding off on the run tonight. She began telling me that my skin color was grayish and white and that I didn't look well. I justified her observations by noting that it was because of this stomach virus that had besieged me. My brother Paul was over visiting with us. He, too, was riding me about the fact that my appearance was sickly and was concerning. My brother and my wife were very insistent that I give it a break and forget the run for the evening. I had one foot out the door into the cold, and she is telling me that perhaps I should call the emergency room and just run my symptoms by them. I kept telling her she was crazy. *Why am I going to call the emergency room and pester them because of a virus?* was my way of thinking. My wife was insistent that I call the local emergency room at the Burbank Hospital and give them a rundown on what's ailing me. We haggled about making the phone call while I was half in the door and half outside the door. So I finally placated her, and while standing there in full running regalia, I removed some of my running gear and made a phone call to the local emergency room. After running down the list of my symptoms to a nurse on the other end of the phone, I was instructed to come to the hospital immediately. Additionally, she also informed me not to drive but to have my wife drive me to the ER. When I questioned the nurse as to why all the panic, she told me that all my symptoms seemed to indicate possible internal bleeding. At that point, my face turned from the pale gray look it already had to a sheet of white.

We arrived at the hospital, and after mentioning that I was the guy from the phone call, I was immediately escorted to a treatment room. The doctor proceeded to do a rectal exam and then informed me that I was bleeding somewhere between my esophagus and rectum. They also drew some blood. Usually, waiting for blood results from the lab while you're in an emergency room can be painstakingly slow. Not in this case; the blood results came back in record time. I'm talking in less than ten minutes, not the usual hour or more. The evidence was in. I had lost two liters of blood—nearly half the blood volume in your body! There are six liters of blood in the human body. The doctor told me that my hematocrit level was perilously low. It should range between 45 percent and 52 percent. My level was 15 percent! In the meantime, as the exam was proceeding, my body started going into shock. All of a sudden, four or five people were working on me at once with a quickened and deliberate pace. My shirt was cut off, and I was patched up to the EKG machine and given intravenous in both arms. I was convulsing with a shivering cold and was covered in one of those tin foil-type blankets. The worst of it was when the doctor inserted a nasal gastrointestinal tube up my nostril. He then proceeded to snake the tube down my throat and into my stomach, all the while being forced to drink a cup of water through a straw in order to swallow the tube! The involuntary gagging was beyond

DIVINE INTERVENTION

discomforting. I wanted that tube out yesterday, and I was continually letting all parties involved know that. I was so uncomfortable with this tube up my nose and down my throat that I wouldn't move my head even an inch. I would only point to the tube whispering, "Take it out!"

I was completely in fear for my life as this controlled chaos was going on all around me. The tube was flowing with the blood from my stomach and into the jar suspended on the wall behind the hospital bed. It looked like a crazy straw. The nurses were very kind, and I realized that I knew the gravity of my own situation. They comforted me and looked directly into my eyes to assure me. They would tell me that I was going to be alright and that I had arrived just in time. The doctor went to apprise my wife of my condition. He had to tell her not to be alarmed and that I was not just there for a stomach flu. He told her that I was hooked up to tubes and machines and to prepare herself for my appearance. He mentioned that I arrived just in time and that "I was not a happy camper." When Pam walked into the room, she instantly broke down in tears at the sight of me. As I mentioned, there were intravenous lines hooked up to both arms. My chest was all patched up with the EKG wires, and I was hooked up to a monitor. There was a nasal gastrointestinal tube up my nose, pumping my stomach. I also had oxygen flowing into my nose from a tube, and I had a foil blanket on me. It was a nightmare!

I can remember the nurses telling my wife that she had gotten me to the hospital just in time. I spent a couple of nights in the ICU and five nights overall in the hospital. The attending physician, who was a gastroenterologist, came to visit me while I was in the hospital. He said that if I had gone for the five-mile run that night, there was a good possibility I may have died. He was willing to bet that within the first mile, I would have suffered a full cardiac event and dropped on the road. He explained to us that I was operating on half a tank of blood in my body. Hence the labored breathing, dizziness, and fatigue. The black, tarry stools were dead blood hemorrhaging from my body. The extra-strength aspirin bored a hole in my small intestine, from which the blood was evacuating my body. The doctor said it was kind of a catch-22. I was in such great physical condition from running and training that I was able to endure many of the symptoms of the internal bleeding. He said, "Being in such great shape almost killed me."

When I think about it now, the one-mile mark of my training route would have placed me on a back road right in the middle of the woods. If I allow my thoughts to wander, I begin to imagine the unimaginable, lying on the pitch-black side of a back road on a freezing cold winter night in the middle of the woods. Perhaps I wouldn't have realized what hit me—a massive heart attack. I would have been struggling to breathe, lying in the cold and dark and shivering, all alone and so afraid. My life is ebbing from

DIVINE INTERVENTION

me, slowly dying and wondering at the tender age of twenty-nine. What is happening to me? Am I dying?

Praise God for my wife's insight and for her intuition. Her insistence could not be ignored. Her instinct was right on. I was on my way out the door! Her suggestion to call the ER seemed foolish to me. I was having no part of it! I had a run to do and sweat to burn. This Boston Marathon was important to me, and keeping with the running schedule was paramount. It was an inconvenience to drop everything and make a silly phone call! My patience was short as I came back in the door and had to remove my gloves, mask, and hat to make the phone call.

Surely, God works in mysterious ways. My time had not yet come. God's Holy Spirit reached out to my wife, who then reached out to me. A supernatural intervention was necessary in order to preserve my life, lest I be left to my own devices. Oh, how gracious and merciful is my heavenly Father! His timing is perfect! Why me, Lord? My heart is full. Thank You a billion times over. Amen!

Take Me Out to the Ball Game

My mother's name was Theresa. She was a Portuguese woman from the old school. In fact, when it came to any formal schooling, she barely had any. She grew up on the backstreets of Cambridge, Massachusetts, along the Charles River. Mom had three brothers and six other sisters. It was a family of ten kids! The days of those large families are a thing of the past. Mom grew up very poor and came to know all she knew from the school of life's experience and hard knocks. I can recall, especially during my teen years, that she would always make the effort to talk about God and Jesus to me and my friends. My siblings and I would always tease her and say, "Here she goes again, Mother Theresa." It was ironic that her name was Theresa and she was indeed our mother. A quaint play on words, I suppose! We really did upset her sometimes when the joke was carried too far. Gosh, if we only knew then what we know now!

DIVINE INTERVENTION

During my senior year of high school, my mom was diagnosed with non-Hodgkin lymphoma. She was also battling full-blown insulin-dependent diabetes. steroids, chemotherapy, three insulin shots a day, and a myriad of medications became the norm. There came a time in the beginning of the cancer that mom was basically sent home from the hospital to be made comfortable and to die. She was not responding to the chemo treatments. I can remember that the situation was dire. Not coming home from my first semester of college was not an option. I came home from college to find my fifty-two-year-old mother situated in the living room, lying in a hospital bed. I was in disbelief, but I could see that she was dying. I was shocked at how she had declined in health while I was away. Suddenly and miraculously, by the grace of God, "Mother Theresa," in the eleventh hour, started responding to the chemotherapy. Not a minute too soon! The chemotherapy was finally working. It was shrinking the tumors! Both my mom and our entire family were given a second chance. For the next nine years, my mother managed to battle both diabetes and non-Hodgkin lymphoma and maintained a reasonably good quality of life.

Eventually, however, the lymphoma managed to outwit and circumvent the chemotherapy. The medicine, a.k.a. poison, was no longer able to keep the tumors shrunken and at bay. At this point, the horrifying downward spiral had begun. The suffering she endured in the last year of her life was merciless! She was hospitalized for weeks and months on end.

She had a stroke, congestive heart failure, and a compromised immune system, to mention only a few things. Poor mom battled through every virus and infection that came along. Most of the time, she was so sick and had a fever due to her inability to resist any of these illnesses.

When mom had the stroke earlier on, it caused a condition known as aphasia. It's the inability to understand or express speech. I remember witnessing the horrifying effects of aphasia firsthand on a visit to the hospital one day. My mother kept pulling the NG (nasal gastrointestinal) tube out of her nose. It was the tube that went up her nose and down into her stomach in order to keep the fluids from building up. The nursing staff would try to communicate with her if she wanted the tube in or the tube out. They would tell her that it was best if the NG tube were left in. The tube would help her feel better. It was pitiful and frustrating to watch as my mom would say, "Want tube in," and then proceed to pull it out once it was reinserted. That fiasco happened twice while I was there. I never felt more helpless. I would ask my mom for her wishes regarding the tube, but it was futile. It was like trying to communicate when you both speak a different language. It was a real bad day! One I will never ever forget. I was lost in despair. How could I make my mom comfortable and rest easy? How could I talk with her, if even just one more time?

Eventually, my mom began to lie back in the upright bed and started to quiet down. I took some

DIVINE INTERVENTION

hand cream and began massaging her arm. She just stared straight ahead with a blank look on her face. All of a sudden, she clutched the side rails of her bed and pulled her emaciated eighty-pound body to a sitting position. She turned to her left and stared intently at me. Her wide eyes pierced mine. I was startled, if not scared! Up until this point, Mom had not been able to communicate anything to me verbally. She gritted her teeth and, in a very stern tone, said to me, "Take me out to the ball game!"

I shook my head and said, "I don't understand."

I asked her what she was trying to say to me. She glared at me with deeper consternation. Her eyes were gazed intently on mine. She mustered the energy and repeated it with an even harsher tone: "TAKE ME OUT TO THE BALL GAME!"

At that point, I was totally confused and distraught by Mom's deteriorating condition. Mom turned from looking at me, and while still in the seated upright position, she stared straight ahead. She had a disgusted and extremely frustrated countenance. She shook her head back and forth in confusion and blew out a long, heavy sigh through her pursed lips. Mom then allowed herself to flop back down hard onto the reclined bed as she released her grip on the side rails. She threw herself back in total disgust. I started to cry and apologized for not being able to understand her. We sat there in despair and in silence. Then, in less than thirty seconds, it was as if a light bulb went on in my head! I abruptly looked at my mom and said, "Do you want to go home,

Mom? Are you trying to tell me that you want to go home?" I will take her response to my grave with me. She nodded her head up and down to say yes, yes, and tears flowed out of her eyes and rolled down her cheeks. I knew she did not want to perish watching a wall-mounted television or staring at a big, round Simplex clock on the wall. My mother wanted to go home, period!

I ran to call my dad on the pay phone. I sadly remember telling him that there was no more light at the end of the tunnel. Mom was dying. He cried hard and was broken as he admitted to the same conclusion. I pleaded with him to get Mommy home. I told him that she had made it very clear to me that she needed to go home now. He said that he would figure it all out and begin to get to work on it. However, he didn't have the same urgency as I did or his dying wife. I said, "No, Dad, NOW!"

The family got together, and we met with hospice. I remained strongly vigilant about the time frame and what Mom made known to me. Dr. Hoffman, Mom's oncologist for the entire ten years of this lymphoma saga, helped to facilitate the move with the hospice care folks. Dr. Hoffman made it very clear to the entire family that my mom would live for another ten days and possibly up to fourteen more days. There was no reason not to trust his professional opinion. In our eyes, our mom's doctor was the best.

We brought Mom home within two days of the message she had conveyed to me. It was a cold

DIVINE INTERVENTION

Wednesday in February 1992. The following day, within twenty-four hours of leaving the hospital, on Thursday, she died in her bedroom in her home. She was on oxygen only, and the entire family watched as she went through those horrible final stages of death. It was a day for me that will live in my mind and heart forever. How can it be? What about the ten days or two weeks! Dr. Hoffman, really! You didn't say one day; you said a minimum ten!

It had nothing to do with Dr. Hoffman's prediction. The good Lord orchestrated the entire plan. He allowed me to be there that horrible day in the hospital, just me and my mom—the day Mom battled the nasal gastrointestinal tube, the day she struggled with aphasia and fear. One thing is abundantly clear: there can be no doubt that the Almighty God in heaven allowed me to understand my mother's intentions. "Take me out to the ball game! Take me out to the ball game!" I heard you, Mom. It took a few seconds, but I heard you because God tuned my ear in, and He opened my mind and heart to know exactly what you meant and wanted. It may have taken me thirty seconds for the light to go on, but I got it.

There was a time previously in the ICU, right after Mom had a heart attack. She had a little plastic gold Jesus taped to the hospital bed. She wasn't really able to communicate well because of the aphasia. I remember asking her if she loved Jesus while I was pointing to Him. She gave me a big, slow, and deliberate nod to indicate a yes. Then I told her not to worry about anything and that Jesus would take care of everything. All my life, she always told me about Jesus, despite my teasing her. Jesus allowed my mom to leave that hospital, go home, and be with her family. We were all there to say goodbye; we assured her that she was a good mom and that it was okay to go. She was in the company of her entire family in the home she loved. Then Jesus brought Mom to His eternal home to live forever. God is wonderful and so gracious. He gave my mom what she wanted, and He allowed the entire family to witness His mighty hand at work. Thank You, God, for that obvious display. Thank You, Lord, for Your always perfect timing. Thank You for opening my eyes to Your presence. Most of all, dear God, thank You for decoding Mom's message for me: "Take me out to the ball game!" Praise be to God!

An Old Friend

had this one particular friend in high school. I'll give him the pseudonym John to protect his identity, of course. We chummed around together every chance we could. John was a somewhat troubled kid. He had a huge chip on his shoulder and wouldn't take any sort of joking around about himself. Even if you were just kidding, you had to tread lightly or face his wrath! On many occasions, John would find himself engaged in knockdowns and drag-out fisticuffs with the best of his fellow men. Too many times, I had to make every attempt to keep the peace and spare us yet another brawl. It got to the point where it wasn't fun anymore to pal around with my old pal John! I, on one hand, was more interested in seeking the attention of the fairer sex, perhaps savoring the taste of cherry lip gloss on my lips. I mean, isn't that what normal high school boys are usually all about? John, on the other hand, was apparently more interested in the taste of blood on his lips! Nearly 100 percent of the time, John got what he wished for, as he would watch his latest poor, unsuspecting adversary limp away with a newly acquired black eye or busted nose. I mean, they were not all poor and unsuspecting. There were certainly that rough and tough handful who welcomed a good hearty go-round with some bare knuckles. Fistfights seemed to find their way to my troubled friend. Not surprisingly, John, it seemed, always came out the victor! Most of John's opponents were summarily humbled and usually retreated with a much-bruised ego and some awful wounds to lick, with one more in the loss column.

During the last couple of years of high school, while we were still close buddies, I began to realize that perhaps a lot of John's anger and aggression were probably due to depression. The more I hung around with John, the more I noticed this destructive behavior. I certainly didn't profess to be a psychologist, but it was becoming readily apparent that there were obvious underlying issues that fueled John's aggression. Most of my longtime friends had watched this go on for quite a while and slowly began to dissociate themselves from me due to my loyal relationship with John. I, however, hung in there, thinking that maybe I could make a difference—wishful thinking at best! Well, John graduated high school the year before me. He moved away, and I went on to college the following fall.

Over the years, John and I lost contact with each other. I occasionally thought about him. I wondered if he ever hung up his vicious brawling habits. As a matter of fact, I questioned whether or not he was still among the living. Perhaps he had crossed the

DIVINE INTERVENTION

wrong person during a hellacious fistfight? Maybe somebody exacted mortal revenge against John for a previous beating they had endured at his hands! For all I knew, he could be languishing in a prison cell for the crime of manslaughter! I sure hoped the years had calmed John down and perhaps tamed his aggression. Maybe he had found some peace with that inner struggle I knew he dealt with. I began to become overly curious about what had become of my old combatant friend. After fifteen years of having no contact with John and pondering what had become of him, I decided to see if I could locate him. I made several phone calls, trying vigorously to track John down. Lo and behold, I was finally able to locate John and actually obtain a contact phone number. It was a beautiful hot summer day, and I was swimming at my dad's pool when the time finally arrived. For whatever reason, I decided that today was the day I would attempt to contact John personally.

I came in from the swimming pool at Dad's house, made my way to the old dial-up phone, sat down, and nervously dialed the number of John. *Ring, ring, ring!* Suddenly, catching me by surprise, the voice on the other end of the phone said, Hello! I said hello as well, and then inquired if it was indeed John that I was speaking to. Believe it or not, I already knew it was him. His voice sounded the same even after fifteen or so years.

"John! This is Joe Cappucci!" His immediate response was very strange, to say the least. I will never forget his reaction. He went into a tirade of hellacious expletives about how he couldn't believe it was me who was calling him.

"Is this really you? I can't believe this is really you on the phone after all these years." There were actually a whole lot of cuss words in between. John was so taken aback by the fact that I had reached out to him. He was literally in disbelief and, quite honestly, somewhat breathless and frantic! The swearing and unbelief were steady and oppressive. As he began to calm down, I questioned him about what was going on—why the crazy reaction?

The great radio broadcaster, Paul Harvey, used to say, "Now you know the rest of the story." John began to divulge to me that just as he was walking in the door from an excursion he was on, the phone was ringing, and it was me. I asked him where he had been. That's when he told me that he just got back from attempting to kill himself. An hour or so previously, he said goodbye to his wife and toddler daughter and actually waved to them as he was pulling out of his driveway. They had no idea where he was going or that he had packed his shotgun in the car. John drove to a field in the woods and was wresting up the nerve to shoot himself. He had explained to me that he had been going through a really rough patch. He also said he had spent some nights in jail and that depression and anxiety were a daily hateful ritual. He mentioned that he no longer felt of any good use to his family and that his being dead would be better for them. He was utterly hopeless! John told me that many times he had the gun in position at the

DIVINE INTERVENTION

ready. Each time he thought he could do it, he was overwhelmed with a feeling of not being able to carry through with this terrible deed. As he attempted it over and over again, the same sense—gut feeling, intuition, or whatever you want to label it—held him back. He began to sob as he relayed the rest of the story to me. After several attempts at ending his life that afternoon, John wept in his car and drove home. As he came into the house, the phone was ringing, and it was an old friend calling. That friend was me!

John unloaded the whole story and all the details of his life leading up to that fateful day. It was tragic and heartbreaking! This was my opportunity to explain to John that there are no such things as coincidences in this life. My heart was full of a sense of awe and compassion. My God-given calling was at the ready. It was now very apparent to me why this phone call had been on my mind for weeks. As often as I tried to dismiss the whole notion of calling John, the conviction was overwhelming. The truth is that I told John that our Creator, God Himself, had purposed this phone call and understood the despair he was experiencing. I relayed to him that God's Spirit was in that field with him today and that God loved him so much! I went on to tell him that I had become a Christian since I had last seen him. I expounded the gospel, good news, and of Jesus to him. The rest of my conversation with John that day centered on the fact that this whole telephone conversation was orchestrated by God in a supernatural way. God was in the details in order to save his life and to invite him to accept Jesus as his Savior. I am a messenger of the good news of salvation through the finished, redemptive work of Christ on the cross. I can't make a person choose to receive Jesus's gift of eternal life. I can only lead them to the one that could bring meaning to their lives. John had free will that day, and regrettably, he politely declined the invitation to come to the one who could both save his life and his eternal soul.

There can be no doubt about the countless efforts, means, and ways God intervenes in everyone's lives. Surely, there is more than just coincidence or happenstance in these most timely events. God, in his love, mercy, and enduring patience, loved John so much that He reached down from heaven that day. He beckoned John to come and find the meaning in his life that he longed so much for. I just happened to be a ready, willing, and able vessel in the plan that God was working on in John's life. God summoned me, an old friend, to reach out to an old friend at the perfect and precise time. What an awesome calling! What a privilege! Who am I to be used in these circumstances? I am but a sinner, saved by grace!

Hawaii Stones

f I haven't mentioned it already, I am a life insurance and annuity sales financial planner. Most of the time, my line of work can be extremely rewarding. I really enjoy helping people with their life insurance portfolio and helping them prepare for their retirement needs as well. The downside of the job is when clients who have become your friends suddenly pass away. Yes, on the one hand, it's good to know that the surviving family members can continue to sustain themselves financially because of the benefits the life insurance proceeds bring. Yet at the same time, the grief is profound due to these untimely deaths. I would like to believe that making my acquaintance and allowing me into their homes to sell them a death benefit certainly made a difference for their families, at least financially. I take comfort in that. There is a rewarding feeling, perhaps knowing that my efforts will be helping a family continue their standard of living or perhaps pay for a future college education.

The job comes with some great perks offered by the insurance company. If your performance numbers meet certain levels of production, you get a paid-in-full, glamorous vacation for a job well done! Fortunately, I've had the pleasure of attending many company conventions over the years, all over the United States. These convention sites were second to none, with luxurious accommodations at five-star resorts! A convention trip would be pretty tough to afford on your own if the insurance company wasn't footing the entire bill, including the airfare.

One such convention site was Maui, Hawaii. In April 1995, my wife and I stayed at the Maui Hyatt Regency! Wow, it was incredible! The hotel was on the Kaanapali Coast. Straight out from the beach to the west was the island of Lanai. It appeared as though it was less than five miles away, yet it was eighteen miles across the channel. What a stunning view! Looking up the beach to the north was the stunning island of Molakai, with its ragged, steep cliffs. It was breathtaking! To the south, you could see the island of Kahoolave. Four Hawaiian islands for the price of one. Clearly, I now know why they call Hawaii paradise! I have had the pleasure of attending many conventions on the insurance company dime. Believe me, they spare no expense. They treat you like royalty. No other convention location has ever topped the Maui convention. The beautiful blue water, tropical breezes, swaying palm trees, hula dancers, luaus, fire breathers, tropical drinks with little umbrellas in them, tiki torches, breeching whales, and, of course, a never-ending supply of fresh pineapple.

DIVINE INTERVENTION

My wife and I were slated to stay for a week in paradise. We really didn't want to spend more than a week in Maui, as we had two small children at home in the care of family members. Oh, did I forget to mention that my wife, Pam, was six months pregnant with our third child?

The end of the week came, and we enjoyed our last night on Maui. Our luggage was all packed up, and we were ready to get some sleep for the early, long flight out in the morning. We were anxious and excited at the same time to get back to our boys and to the routine of real life. Pam and I exchanged kisses good night and our nightly I love you, then drifted off.

The morning came, and I was out like a light. The proverbial coma. The festivities of the week and all the travel had taken their toll on me. I awoke to be alone in bed. Suddenly, I was roused by my wife's faint, distant cries. I startled out of bed and ran to the bathroom, only to find my pregnant wife sitting on the shower floor, water pouring over her head, and crying in horrible pain while vomiting uncontrollably. She told me she was calling out for me for over half an hour! That killed me! I didn't hear her cries over the running shower and because of the exhausted deep sleep I was in. I got her out of the shower, dialed 911, dried her off, and dressed her. The 911 call alerted the hotel manager to our room. Almost immediately, he was knocking on the door. He came into the room with other staff, and soon the EMTs arrived. It was *crazy*! Everybody present was somewhat in a panic.

Poor Pam! Her pain was excruciating. It was coming from her right flank on the lower back. The ambulance rushed her to Maui Memorial Hospital in Wailuku, Maui, with me riding shotgun. When we got to the hospital, the doctor was quick to inject her with painkillers; Dilaudid comes to mind. I remember telling him that my wife was pregnant, and I was concerned about the baby getting those drugs in his or her body. It was decided that keeping the mother out of pain was the first priority and ultimately best for the baby as well. I was so worried for my wife and unborn child! I was experiencing high anxiety. I was at my wits end. We were now five thousand miles away, stuck on Maui. Our boys were home missing us; we were missing them terribly, and our flight back to normal family life had now come and gone. To make matters worse, all our belongings were forty-five minutes away, stuffed into luggage on the other side of the island at the hotel—a hotel that we were now checked out of. In addition, I was down to my last few dollars. I know it seems crazy, but I didn't even own a credit card!

My beautiful, pregnant, and tanned wife was admitted to Maui Memorial Hospital in Wailuku, Maui, Hawaii. She was kept sedated the entire time, and her diagnosis was kidney stones! All I could think about was my wife's discomfort and whether or not our baby was going to be alright.

When Pam was moved into a room, I went with her and remained by her side vigilantly. It was my job to make sure she was out of pain and resting comfort-

DIVINE INTERVENTION

ably. That meant politely keeping after the nurses to bring her the pain medication every time she would stir out of sleep and begin wincing in extreme discomfort. I was as polite as I could be and always remembered to say please and thank you. After all, I was their guest on their island and in their hospital. I had also come to discover that visiting hours were till eight o'clock at night.

The head of hospital security stopped by the room while Pam was asleep. He called me outside into the hallway and made certain to remind me that I had to leave at 8:00 p.m. promptly. He was very straightforward, almost without expression. The way he acted toward me was somewhat hostile. I began to think he had something against me. Maybe he didn't like Italians, or perhaps he didn't like Massachusetts. When I explained my situation—pregnant wife, no credit card, no money, no luggage, and checked out of the hotel with no place to go—he could have cared less! I explained to him that in Massachusetts, this would not be the kind of treatment I would receive. In fact, I said, the hospital would usually provide a cot if they had one or would allow me to sleep in the chair. This man was downright mean, with zero compassion or sympathy! He educated me that we were not in Massachusetts and reiterated that he would come by around eight o'clock to make sure I was on my way. For whatever reason, this man was adamant about making sure I vacated the building at 8:00 p.m. He absolutely stonewalled me! I had the distinct impression that this guy really enjoyed his position of power and, even more so, being a bully as well. What had I done wrong? Up until that time, I falsely assumed the hospital staff would accommodate me, staying with my very pregnant and now fully-sedated wife. Never assume. My bad!

I was overcome with worry. My anxiety was peaking toward panic. I felt terribly alone and helpless to help my wife or myself. I was worried about our kids back home as well. There would have to be the juggling of schedules, rides to and from school, and who was going to be able to take care of them. What about the flight cancellation and the rescheduling of a new flight? For what day would I schedule the flight home? I had no idea when my wife would be fit to travel! Where was I going to stay until Pam could travel again? What was I going to do? It seemed like the weight of the world was on my shoulders. Eight o'clock was looming ever closer, like a death sentence! Everything seemed to be crashing down on me. *God, please help me! I need You! I'm scared! What should I do?*

I left my hallway meeting with the self-appointed hospital landlord and headed back to my wife's bedside. She was sleeping comfortably. I sat there bewildered at this predicament I now found myself in. I sat quietly, looking out the window toward the nearby steep mountains in the distance. I began to ponder my options as to where I would go after visiting hours ended. My first thought was to hang around the hospital grounds and maybe just pass out on a bench and repeat the same each night

DIVINE INTERVENTION

till it was time to catch a flight. I suppose, for the time being, I was homeless. I remember thinking that at least the weather couldn't be any nicer.

As I walked around the hospital grounds looking for a suitable perch for the night, I was overwhelmed with one thought: over and over again, like a broken record, was the word hospital administrator. The notion was inescapable! I couldn't get the thought out of my brain. It was so specific. *Go see the hospital administrator! Find the hospital administrator.* It was my new quest. So I sought out and found the directory of physicians in the hospital's main lobby. I scanned it up and down, left and right, until my eyes came to focus on one name. That name was Marion L. Hanlon, MD, hospital administrator. Why had the idea of the hospital administrator so captured my thoughts? I was about to find out. Could this man be the help I was so desperately in need of?

I made my way into the elevator and headed up toward the office of Dr. Marion L. Hanlon. I somewhat reluctantly approached the office door and peered in. A woman was sitting behind a desk, and there was an office in the rear of the room. As I looked in the room, she inquired if she could help me. I asked her if Dr. Hanlon, the "hospital administrator," was in. To my surprise, an elderly man came walking out of the back office. He appeared to be around seventy years old or so. He was tired-looking and hunched over. This man had such a gentle spirit about him as he slowly made his way toward me and shook my hand. He was very kind and asked how he could be of help. By this time, my emotions and anxiety were begging to give way to tears. My emotions were welling up inside me, and I didn't want them to burst out like a waterfall. Dr. Hanlon could sense my anguish; he was compassionate. For the moment, my composure was in check. I pushed the tears away and then pushed through all the details of our kidney stone drama. I also made certain to tell him about the head of security and my dealings with him.

What Dr. Hanlon did next, I will remember all the days of my life! He asked me to walk with him through the hospital grounds. We made our way behind the hospital to some condominium housing on the property. Apparently, these condos were owned by the hospital and used for visiting doctors, nurses, and even hospital staff. Dr. Hanlon brought me over to one, took out a key, and opened the door. He handed me the key and said I was welcome to stay as long as needed. At that point, I was ready to move to Maui! Just kidding! Dr. Hanlon reached into his pocket and handed me a meal ticket pass to the hospital cafeteria; he also asked me if I needed any money. I politely declined and said he had already done so much for me. This gentle, kind, and aged man then put his arm around me and asked me if he could pray for me. If I wasn't crying yet, I most certainly was by the time he finished his prayer. His kind, sweet, and needful words pierced to the core of my being. My heart was laid wide open, and the tears streamed down my cheeks. He beseeched God on my behalf, asking Him to heal Pam, protect our

DIVINE INTERVENTION

unborn baby, watch over the boys at home, and give me peace and assurance. All the emotions I was bottling up through this ordeal came through in a torrent. There was no holding back as I sobbed for my wife, my unborn child, and a little for me, I guess. Dr. Hanlon's loving, steady arm around me was like a warm blanket on a freezing, cold February night back in Massachusetts. He promised me that he would look in on Pam and me as well. I felt the presence of Jesus that afternoon. He was inside Dr. Hanlon, ministering to me. Oh, what a joy! Oh, what a magnificent blessing!

What a relief! I left Pam's bedside with confidence that things would be okay. Believe it or not, the hospital security guy showed up on time as promised. I walked past him as I left her hospital room with my hope fully restored. I actually had a decent night's sleep, except for being freaked out by the occasional little gecko scuttling across the wall or ceiling above my bed in the condo.

The next morning, the hotel manager from the Maui Hyatt Regency met me in the hospital lobby with a huge, beautiful bouquet of flowers. He also had all our luggage in tow. I instantly recognized him. This was the same gentleman that was first on scene in the hotel room the morning before. At the time, I was amazed at this incredibly kind gesture. He told me that he put us on his church prayer list and to expect church members to get in touch with me via the hospital room telephone. They wanted to offer any assistance possible to my wife and me.

In addition, he told me that his hotel staff would be working every day and night to reschedule our flights home. My only job was to call them every morning and let them know my wife's medical status. People were calling, offering their cars to me for the day. Some folks even asked if I wanted to be picked up for dinner at a local establishment or even come to their house for a meal. Some folks came by to visit and chat. The people from that church were going out of their way to make sure that Pam and I were okay. Dr. Hanlon's wife, Amy, even paid a visit to Pam!

Pam stayed in the hospital for four days. The Maui Hyatt Regency arranged our flights home. It was really tough going; Pam was weak, still in some pain, and feeling drugged. We got to the airport via a ride arranged by the hotel. Yet another wonderful gesture. We think my wife actually passed a stone at the airport. The flight was a red-eye through the night with one stop in San Francisco. We stayed on the plane while other passengers deplaned and some boarded. Pam took some medication for the flight home, and we managed to survive this whole ordeal. Who would have thought that paradise, in the end, would have morphed into a nightmare?

Is it really true? Can it be real? Can we actually speak words out of our hearts, words that don't necessarily even have to be aloud, and yet God responds? Is there a supernatural presence in the universe that is coherent and intimately responsive to the needs of human beings? If the answers to these questions are yes, then that begs another question: is our Creator

DIVINE INTERVENTION

waiting and poised to do good things on our behalf? My response to each question is a resounding yes! There can be no doubt in my mind and heart that God was with Pam and me on the island of Maui, Hawaii! He responded to my cries. He heard my plea for help. He understood my fears and anxiety. God knew my son in his mother's womb, and every hair on his head was numbered. Anthony was fearfully and wonderfully knitted together inside his mom. I will be forever thankful to Dr. Hanlon for responding to God's leading in our little crisis. My heart is full of joy every time I recall those days at Maui Memorial Hospital.

It would be three years later, on July 20, 1998, that Dr. Marion Hanlon died of pulmonary fibrosis. I know this because his loving wife, Amy, sent me a beautiful Christmas card. On the cover was a palm tree with Christmas bulbs on it that read, Aloha at Christmas. Inside was a sweet note. She told me of Dr. Hanlon's disease and of his passing. Mrs. Amy Hanlon confided that she missed Marion and that she was struggling with loneliness. Amy said that she knew Dr. Hanlon was experiencing ultimate joy as he was enjoying being with his Lord and Savior! The last thing Mrs. Hanlon mentioned in her note was to ask whether we had had a boy or girl.

On a side note, our son Anthony was born back in Massachusetts four months later, in August. He was perfectly healthy and happy. He did, however, have a congenital heart defect. He was born with a bicuspid aortic valve instead of the normal tricuspid. He has been monitored since birth on a regular basis and is quite healthy with no limitations. Was this defect caused by the medications given to Pam in the hospital? Doctors say no, indicating that the heart was fully developed by the time she went in for the kidney stones. I guess we'll never know this side of eternity. Incidentally, Anthony has had severe kidney stones on at least three occasions, twice requiring three and five days of hospitalization. Crazy huh! I guess the apple doesn't fall far from the tree. I will see you on the other side, Dr. Marion Hanlon! Give Jesus a kiss for me; thanks again!

Under the Trestle

Most folks will think it's crazy, but I often pick up hitchhikers. I guess I'm partial to lending a ride because, in my earlier days of youth, thumbing a ride was a staple. I thumbed everywhere! More often than not, these folks have fallen on hard times. They may have a mental illness that prevents them from driving, or sometimes they have gotten into trouble with the law because of a DWI or OUI. Other times, these folks just don't have the financial means to own a car. I just feel compelled to lend a ride and get them nearer to where they are headed. I'm not concerned with safety; it's really not an issue to me. I have never experienced even an iota of trouble, only extreme gratitude from my passenger.

I was out and about one summer day, driving west in Groton, Massachusetts. As you begin to head out of town, you pass under this old train trestle. Nowadays, the state has converted it to rails-to-trails, which are walked and biked on and enjoyed by many folks. Standing under this trestle was a rather peculiar-looking middle-aged man. He was holding a sign that read, Greenville, NH. That was his desired destination; it was roughly fifteen to twenty miles away. This man had a very strange look to him, which, in my opinion, appeared as though he may have a mental or emotional illness. I was somewhat apprehensive about taking on this passenger and decided to pass on this one. I actually drove past him for about half a mile and felt good about my decision. However, I soon relented to my conscience, turned around, and headed back up to the trestle, where he was still standing with his handmade magic marker sign.

I was now across the road from him and rolled down my window to advise him that I was going to cross the road and give him a ride. He gladly accepted, and we were on our way. I struck up a conversation and asked if he was from Groton and what his name was. I went to high school in Groton, and as it turned out, my new passenger was the brother of a friend who graduated with me. The age difference between my friend and his older brother was quite a spread. For this reason, I didn't know him. What a small world!

The one thing I am not is shy, so the conversation rolls pretty easily off my lips. I told my passenger—let's call him Dave—that his brother and I were good friends and played little league together as youngsters. So the next question I asked was right to the heart of the matter: why is it that you don't drive? I was expecting the usual DWI response, but instead Dave informed me that he had a seizure disorder. He wasn't willing to take a chance on driving and poten-

DIVINE INTERVENTION

tially hurting himself or others if a seizure should occur. Now I was getting nervous. My next question was more out of a need to quell my nerves! When was the last time you had a seizure? I was glad to hear that it was over two years ago and that medication was keeping the problem in check. In addition, Dave told me that he usually knows when he is about to have a seizure. Phew, my nervous system calmed from a seven to a two. Dave and I shared pleasantries over the next few miles as we got closer to my hometown of Townsend, Massachusetts.

We weren't twenty-five yards past the Townsend town line sign when Dave started convulsing in a full-blown grand mal seizure! How can this be happening! He was flopping wildly, and his arms and legs were banging on the dashboard and side door panel. All the while, he was drooling and had just completely succumbed to this malicious malady! I pulled my car over to the side of the road and took my keys out of the ignition. I turned toward the passenger seat and spoke very deliberately to Dave in a calmer than calm voice. As I monitored Dave and made sure he was safe, I began to tell him he was not alone and he would be taken care of. The seizure lasted about two to three minutes. I don't know if Dave heard anything that was said to him during the seizure. When the seizure ended, he was absolutely exhausted and slouched over in the seat. He had no recollection of how long he seized for. I asked Dave if we should proceed to the hospital, as my intention was to bring him to the nearest emergency room.

JOSEPH CAPPUCCI

Dave asked me how long the seizure lasted as he wiped saliva from his mouth and breathed heavily. I was extremely concerned for him, but he said if the seizure didn't last more than ten minutes, there would be no need to go to the emergency room. At this point, I was a little in shock and was tempted to take Dave to the local ER despite his objection. There was no way I was leaving him off at my destination only to have to hitchhike the balance of his way home. No way! We compromised, and I insisted that we head directly to his house. The extra five or six miles it would take to get there was an insignificant drive. My only thought was getting Dave to his house safely.

I walked Dave to his door. He was very weak and exhausted, even somewhat confused, yet he was insisting he was alright. When Dave was in his house and out of sight, I immediately made a covert telephone call. I was able to track down his father's telephone number and make a call. I remembered Dave's dad from my youth, as he always showed up at our little league games. At the time of this call, I would guess he was in his seventies, Dave was in his fifties, and I was in my thirties. I apprised him of his son's seizure and that he seemed to be doing alright and was now at home. I really wanted to make sure that Dave didn't need to be at a hospital. His father couldn't be more thankful for me helping his son out. He also indicated that he remembered me graduating with his other son and that it was nice chatting with me.

DIVINE INTERVENTION

What are the chances! I didn't want to give this guy a ride. I was kind of weirded out by his manner and appearance under the trestle. I passed him by half a mile, yet I was compelled to go back and give him a ride despite feeling a little apprehensive. He hadn't had a seizure in over two years and was under good control on medicine. The real deal is that Dave was right where he was supposed to be, and I was right where I was supposed to be. God, in His sovereignty, arranged for me to be Dave's caretaker that day. God's Spirit moved me to turn about and take care of the need at hand. You can call it a coincidence if you want to. Although, after a while, coincidences stop being coincidences. Sometimes one has only to look about and be sensitive to the particular needs of another human being. God's Spirit will let you know when the time is right and what the right thing to do is. When an event like this happens and the Dave situations arise in life, you just know it's the Lord's doing. Go with it and be joyous over being blessed and called as a vessel or agent of God's will. Be humbled to say, *Why me, Lord? Who am I but a mere human!* God is supernatural, and He orchestrates supernatural timing at various times and places. When the situation you find yourself in comes to a close, just give thanks and praise for being part of a divine intervention!

Backpack Nomad

Did I mention already that I'm in the habit of picking up hitchhikers? I guess I have a knack for spying out situations where some folks could use a little help. Perhaps it's an addiction. In my case, I truly believe it's somewhat part of my calling. So many folks are down and out and just need a little grace to get by. I guess that's where I come in. I'm a big softy when I see someone on the side of the road looking anxious and desperate to get somewhere. I've been in their shoes countless times in my life and know intimately what it feels like. So yet another bizarre hitchhiking account begins!

I arose early one weekday morning as I had an appointment to discuss life insurance with a prospective client in Chelmsford, Massachusetts. My prospect was actually a pastor, and our appointment was for nine that morning. It would take about a forty-five-minute drive through back roads to get there. As it were, I was running a little late and arrived in Chelmsford at about five past nine. I was anxious because I detest being late and was struggling to

DIVINE INTERVENTION

find the physical address. Of course, this was before a Garmin GPS mount on the windshield or GPS directions on a cell phone. I was frantically scanning street names and looking down at an atlas map book, all the while looking like a bobblehead doll. I was getting more desperate with each minute that passed by the nine o'clock hour. Suddenly, I saw a young guy on the opposite side of the road. He was in his mid-twenties with a beard and a backpack. I might add that he appeared somewhat weary. I rolled down the window and yelled across the street to him to see if he knew where such and such a street was. I figured he was a Chelmsford native.

This young man walked over to my car window and replied that he didn't know that address and, in fact, wasn't from around the area. He then turned the tables on me and asked if I knew of a restaurant locally where he could work for a breakfast meal. He made sure to emphasize that it couldn't be some fast-food chain, like McDonald's or Burger King, but had to be a legit establishment where he could perhaps work for his meal by washing dishes or by doing some other menial task. Not being from Chelmsford, I replied that I wasn't sure but could get him a little further down the road, where there were some potential food establishments. So enter the car, my new passenger, all excited about getting off his feet and being driven to his potential morning meal. We chatted a bit about who he was and what his plans were. He said he was from out west, California, actually, and just hitching across the country, landing where he may without any certain plans. "I guess I'm kind of a wandering nomad" was his claim to fame. I drove a bit and was nearing the street I had to turn on in order to find my client's house. I pulled off on the side of the road and mentioned that I felt bad not being able to get him to where he had to go, but I was running late for my appointment. With that said, I reached into my wallet and gave him a sum of money, exclaiming that breakfast and lunch were on me. Please note that I don't say that as a brag or with misplaced pride; it's just who I am and what I do. It's only money! The Spirit leads, and I follow.

My newfound friend was overjoyed and proceeded to break into a conversation about his grandfather. He knew I was in a rush and was concise with his story. He said he respected and loved his granddad so much and that he was a wonderful man and a veteran. He then proceeded to reach into his backpack and handed me a trinket on a chain he claimed he received from his granddad. It was an American flag. I insisted that I couldn't take this from him, but he insisted that I must, as he attempted to equate me with being like his granddad. I was humbled and didn't want to insult him, so I took the gift, and we parted ways with a handshake and a God bless.

As I was driving to my appointment, just a short way down the road, I began to pray earnestly. I felt a deep conviction that perhaps I should have done more for this young man. It was overwhelming! I asked God to help this man and meet his needs along the way. I remember specifically praying and asking

DIVINE INTERVENTION

God to send someone across his path that could take care of this young man and meet his precise needs. I arrived at my appointment fifteen minutes tardy but was able to solve their life insurance needs and had a successful meeting with the pastor and his wife. While I was in the Chelmsford area, I met a few other clients and did some prospecting as well. I also accomplished some errands throughout the day.

Later that day, I headed home. It was around five o'clock in the afternoon on a beautiful, sunny, hot summer evening. I was actually driving on the exact stretch of Route 119 in Groton, Massachusetts, where I picked up my last hitchhiker from the previous chapter. You remember the guy who had the seizure? In fact, it was no more than a few hundred feet down the road, past the trestle. I was driving along, tired from a long day on the road. I had no specific thoughts on my mind save to get home to the wife and kids and have a nice home-cooked dinner. Lo and behold! I see a person thumbing on the roadside ahead of me. I stared at this person intently as I drove past him. I had to do a double take and look in my rearview mirror. I pulled over up ahead and was saying to myself, *No way! This can't be!* I'm thinking *I must be seeing things!* It was the same kid from eight hours ago and almost four towns and twenty-five miles away! I literally thought, *Am I imagining this?*

He approached the opened passenger window and looked in the car. To my utter astonishment, it was him, the California nomad! I said to him, "Aren't you the guy I picked up this morning at nine in Chelmsford?"

He looked at me and replied, "I thought you looked familiar as you drove by." I was freaked out, to say the least! I invited him back into the car, and we were both in disbelief over this chance happening and the whole timing of the matter. It was surreal!

My new, old hitchhiker acquaintance hopped in and set his backpack at his feet. I couldn't notice how weary and exhausted he looked. He was sunburnt, and you could see the dried white spit on the corners of his mouth. Apparently, he was walking all day in the hot sun, attempting to catch rides to continue on his nomadic path. Luckily, I had an extra bottle of water in the car and offered it to him. He sighed a long sigh of relief as he found comfort and rest in sitting in a seat and taking a break from his all-day trek.

As we drove along, I couldn't help but ask him again about what his game plan was. He was, once again, looking for some place to earn a meal. I think he realized we were in the country, so he asked if there were any big cities nearby where he could find a restaurant to work at and garner a meal. It became clear to me that this was his modus operandi for survival while on his cross-country journey. I can only imagine how many floors he swept, dishes he washed, or trash he hauled to a dumpster in order to gain another day's sustenance. It sure seemed to be a tough gig, to say the least. As our conversation continued, I mentioned that there was a city nearby my home where he could perhaps find what he was looking

DIVINE INTERVENTION

for. So off we headed to Fitchburg, Massachusetts. It would be only fifteen to twenty minutes out of my way. No big deal!

Driving along with my weary passenger, I suddenly became overwhelmed with a sense of sadness. His dry, cracked lips and the dried spit on the corners of his mouth really got to me. Maybe it was compassion or sympathy. Given all the years I thumbed over the highways and byways, perhaps it was empathy. I'm not really sure; maybe it's a combination of all the above. At any rate, my emotions were starting to get the best of me. I couldn't stop the thoughts in my head. I wanted to do for this young man anything he needed. My thoughts actually began to worry me, as I felt that perhaps there wasn't going to be a limit to what I was prepared to do. It was a feeling and a thought from the bottom of my stomach to the top of my head. It was like a Nike slogan saying, "Just do it!" Only it was so compelling that I was about to blurt out an open-ended question to my rider with the thought in mind that I would do whatever was asked of me.

In my mind, I literally said, *Well, here goes!* I asked if there was anything he needed and could wish for right now in his life, what would it be? I even repeated the question. His response threw me for a loop and saddened me at the same time. "I would love only to have one good night's sleep." What? I asked where he slept last night. His reply was that he slept up under a bridge. "What about the night before that?" I asked. An open field came his response. It seemed to make sense to me as I looked at his exhausted, dehydrated appearance. Wow, was all I could mutter! The voice in my head was telling me to take care of him. Stop at nothing, and take care of him!

I'll get you to where you want to go was my reply. In my heart of hearts, I wanted to take care of this young man to the tee. So in my mind, I actually came up with the plan to drive him to my home and introduce him to my wife and four kids. She would probably be in shock, as there would be no prior notice of my spur-of-the-moment endeavor. The kiddies would more than likely be huddled in quiet fear. I had it all planned out in my mind. I would offer him a shower if he wanted, feed him dinner, and provide the couch, some blankets, and pillows. Crazy as it may seem, I actually got to where I turned right into my street, and then a moment of clarity hit me like a ton of bricks as I passed my own driveway. There's another way to take care of him. Perhaps this wasn't such a good idea to bring a nomadic stranger home to your family unannounced. While en route to my home, the idea seemed grandiose. As I passed my own driveway, I felt a sense of caution. "An ounce of prevention is worth a pound of cure" seemed to cross my mind. So I exited my neighborhood and headed down the road to Fitchburg, Massachusetts, approximately fifteen to twenty minutes south. We had a casual conversation as we rode along, but my passenger seemed more inclined to rest a spell until we reached the destination.

DIVINE INTERVENTION

Please understand something: at the risk of being misunderstood for bragging or having any heavenly reward burnt up, suffice it to say, my young, nomadic hitchhiker's needs were fully met. He was able to enjoy a warm bed, dinner, dessert, and the following morning's breakfast.

What are the odds! Twice in one day, hours and miles apart. God is the grand orchestrator! What a privilege to be the one to help that young man and see to it that his needs were met! My own earnest prayer that morning that God would bring someone across his path to meet his need was answered meticulously. Who would have ever thought that that someone would be me yet again? It's humbling to the core when you realize the Creator of the universe is calling you for a task. I don't have any great abilities. Why me? God is more interested in availability than ability. I sometimes wonder, actually a lot, about the verse of scripture in the book of Hebrews in the New Testament. In chapter 13, verse 2, it says, "Do not neglect to show hospitality to strangers, for by doing so some people have shown hospitality to angels without knowing it." That is a mind-blowing verse to me. Angels walk among us; it's true! Perhaps my California wandering nomad was an angel. Maybe he was a test for me to determine just how much responsibility God could trust me with. Would I respond to future callings and circumstances? Would I be ready, willing, and pleased to serve our God for His purposes and for His glory? Being in the Lord's army is not always easy and can require personal sacrifice on all levels, such as family, financially, socially, physically, mentally, spiritually, and emotionally, as we shall soon see.

Wheelbarrow

I t was a gorgeous late October day—October 23, 2009, to be exact. Autumn was in full swing, and the red, yellow, and orange colors were nothing less than spectacular to behold. The beautiful scenery was the model of which those seasonal calendars are made. The temperature and the quiet stillness were perfect on this warm and sunny day. There is nothing like fall in New England. Even Barry Manilow has been known to sing about it! It's the reason why people flock to the north in the autumn in order to behold the splendor of creation. The leaf peepers come out in droves to cruise through the countryside and witness this pre-winter splendor of dying leaves.

On this particular beautiful fall day, I decided to head to the gym for a rigorous physical workout. As is usual, I mixed up my potent pre-workout drink. You know, the ones loaded with caffeine and blended with a variety of proprietary herbs and mysterious ingredients. At my age, I figure I could use all the help I can get. An edge, if you will, to get a great workout done. At any rate, the tasty, fruitful blend gives me the boost I'm looking for. With the gym about fifteen to twenty minutes away, it's the perfect time to gulp it down and head out the door. By the time I arrive at the gym, I'm usually all systems go and itching to get busy.

I was making my way to the gym over the back roads of my hometown of Townsend, Massachusetts. As it were, I was running late to meet up with my workout partner. I also had dinner plans with my wife for the evening. These two timely commitments had me feeling somewhat anxious about getting everything done in a timely manner. I'm sure the pre-workout drink might have had something to do with it also.

I was driving up this very long hill, and as I crested the top, the road began to flatten out. I could begin to feel the caffeine kicking in while cruising along, listening to my favorite music. Suddenly, I noticed a rather old gentleman pushing a wheelbarrow on the left-hand side of the road. I was looking out my driver's side window at him walking this wheelbarrow filled with three full, large yard bags inside. The bags were filled with leaves. What caught my immediate attention was the pace of his gait. It had me both dumbfounded and intrigued, to the point where I couldn't look away. Certainly, you would expect an elderly man to have a real slow pace while doing anything, for that matter. However, this man was stepping, better yet shuffling, even creeping, maybe an inch or two with each step. I could not believe what I was seeing! I was so taken aback

DIVINE INTERVENTION

by this that as I passed him, I continued to observe him in my side-view mirror and ultimately through my rearview mirror. It just didn't seem possible that someone could really physically walk that slowly. My thoughts juggled back and forth between that's crazy and whatever, the gym is waiting!

For approximately the next two miles, a war began to rage in my mind, conscience, or spirit, whatever you want to call it. I can claim with complete sanity that I wasn't hearing audible voices in my car, but they were most definitely in my head. The very still and quiet voice was telling me to go back and lend a hand to the old guy. The voice continued, *Surely he could use your help; look at how slow his pace is! What if it were your own father inching along?* The voice nudged. That's when things went from hearing calm suggestions in my mind to me having an audible, mildly angry conversation in the open air of my car.

Please, God, *not* today! I'm late for my meeting at the gym with my workout pal. I have dinner plans with my wife tonight. I'm on this pre-workout drink and starting to feel the buzz. I need to move—places to go, people to see! I will not be delayed! I'm off the clock today, *period*! Get someone else! I will *not* be burdened with this task—not today!

Lo and behold, as determined as I was to make my very valid point known, I lost the argument. After about two miles of both silent and oral debate, I turned my car about-face and headed back to the old-timer. Of course, by now, he had gained about five yards since I originally passed him. Let that sink in! Two miles passed him, and two miles back to him and he gained almost no ground with his less than snail's pace.

I pulled my car alongside him on the side of the road, rolled my passenger window down, and leaned over the front seat in his direction. With my head tilted sideways, I looked straight into his eyes. The old man looked down at me curiously, while I looked up at him with a sense of compassion, curiosity, and wonder. What came out of my lips were the words, "Sir, if you wouldn't mind too much, I would love to give you a hand with that wheelbarrow!"

His immediate response was to say, "Sure, that would be great!"

In the next second, I said, "Hold that thought," and then parked my car in some stranger's driveway on that side of the road. So away we went. My new friend and I crossed the road together and headed toward his house. I told him my name was Joe, and we commented on what a beautiful day it was. He told me his name was Victor, and he commented about how nice of me it was to stop and lend a hand. I believe he used the term fine young man or something like that. He then reached into his wheelbarrow to grab one of the bags of dry leaves. I grabbed the bag back from his hand and said, "Sir, I got this; it's my pleasure!" I got the feeling he was trying to help out in order to feel useful.

We entered his dirt driveway, and I viewed his home for the first time. Well, not exactly the first time.

DIVINE INTERVENTION

I had driven past it hundreds of times over the years. I actually thought it was abandoned. Admittedly, I was somewhat shocked. The house was built on pylons, roughly twelve inches off the ground, with no cellar. It was a very old, worn-down house. The siding was made of asphalt roofing shingles. It was in really rough shape. You could easily describe it as a borderline shack! It appeared almost uninhabitable.

Victor's driveway was comprised of sand and rock. He didn't have all the modern conveniences of a new home, nor did he have a tar driveway. As I made my way to the front of his house with the wheelbarrow, he lagged behind me, still near the beginning of the driveway. I was approximately thirty to forty feet ahead of him, in large part due to his aforementioned snail's pace. All of a sudden, it became very clear to me what the purpose of these bags of leaves was! Victor was using the leaves to fill in the space between the ground and the bottom of the house. It was all about insulating the crawl space around the entire house to keep out the coming cold winter air from moving under the crawl space. It was good ole Yankee ingenuity!

I turned to Victor and mentioned that I understood what he was doing with the leaves. I yelled back to him, "It looks like you have the front of the house done! Can I make my way to the side or back of the house with the wheelbarrow?"

He robustly shouted back to me, "That would be great!" I turned away and started my way toward the side of the house. I took literally one footstep with the wheelbarrow, and at that moment, both of our lives changed in an instant.

I heard a very loud *thud*! When I turned to see Victor, he was face down in the dirt driveway. I immediately rolled my eyes toward the skies and pleaded with God: *Please, Jesus, help me with this one!*

When I got to Victor, he was face down in his driveway! He had dirt in his mouth, nose, ears, and eyes. His forehead was split open and was bleeding. Sand was all in his wound, mixed with oozing blood. He was a bald man, and his entire head was completely blue in appearance. With my limited knowledge of medical things, I suspected he was bleeding subdermally or intercranially. My mind was racing, and I was experiencing high anxiety and borderline panic.

As I watched Victor on the ground with his face in the dirt, one word instantly darted through my brain! The word was dignity. I was not going to allow this man to die on my watch with his face in the dirt. No way, no how! I was fighting back my emotions. I had to help my newfound friend. I proceeded to get on my knees and roll Victor to his right side, facing me. As I scooted up close to him, my right hip was now against his waist. I reached over and put my arm around him and my hand on his back. I'm not going to lie. I was a wreck! I knew he was dying and very near death. I rubbed his back up and down, from the small of his back to the nape of his neck. I kept reassuring him that I was there with him. He was on his right side; his neck was craned toward me, and he

DIVINE INTERVENTION

was looking right into my eyes. This was the second time our eyes met. The first was when I looked up at him from my car. His mouth was opening and closing very slowly for a minute or two. I suspected that he was taking his last breaths, and this was a dying reflex. It was as though he was trying to utter some words to me.

After kneeling there with him for a couple of minutes, I had to run back to my car across the street in order to retrieve my cell phone. I ran as fast as my legs could carry me. I felt terribly guilty, and I still do to this day, for leaving Victor all alone, even just for those few seconds. It was necessary in order to call emergency services. When I got back to Victor, I resumed rubbing his back and telling him it was okay, all the while having a conversation with an EMS operator. Suddenly, his mouth stopped moving, and everything came to a stop. I laid him flat on his back and put my fingers to his neck in order to detect a pulse on his carotid artery and found none. I put my ear to his chest, listening for a heartbeat, only to hear silence. I sat there with Victor, lying on his back in the driveway, for what seemed like an eternity of quiet. Shortly after, a local volunteer firefighter that I know named Gary showed up in the driveway, and we both began CPR efforts. After quickly unwrapping a protective guard that I put over Victor's nose and mouth, I began breathing air into his lungs. Gary did the chest compressions. I recall glancing at Gary with a look of futility and hopelessness on my face. All I could say to Gary is, "Why are we doing this?"

It was abundantly clear to me that life had ended for Victor, and there was no need for additional herculean efforts. Nothing inside me even remotely hinted at performing any life-saving measures. As we continued CPR, Gary's reply was that we had to try!

After several minutes, the ambulance arrived, and they took Victor away. I was later told that the hospital was able to get his pulse going and keep him alive for just a short while longer. However, he was comatose and very near death. It was also told to me that a relative was able to be in his presence and say goodbye. I have heard that when a person is near death in a comatose state, hearing is the last thing to fail. We can only hope that perhaps Victor heard this final farewell before he passed away shortly after.

I stood alone in silence, watching the ambulance drive away. I was in shock, not knowing what to think or how to act. It was like the calm after the storm. Time was on hold for the moment, at a standstill. Should I continue on to the gym or go home and tell my wife what just transpired? I found myself looking at the ground where Victor laid and couldn't help but meander around for a moment in disbelief. I had to look up to observe an elderly woman approaching me. My guess is that she was in her mid-eighties. "Excuse me," she said. "Are you the young man who was with Victor when he died?"

She could tell I was very shaken up and nearing an emotional outbreak. I replied that I was with Victor from the moment I parked my car in the driveway across the street. I went on to tell her my

DIVINE INTERVENTION

name and that I lived in Townsend as well. What's more, I told her I was a Christian and that initially I drove two miles past Victor. Surely, this man *must* have been a Christian, I blurted out! Tell me he was a Christian! I told her that there could be no other way. How can it be that I drove two miles past him and was convicted to come back and lend a hand? How could it be that in those fifteen or so minutes since we met, he died on me? Again, I pleaded, he must have been a Christian man, right? I just can't see it any other way! I was sounding repetitive as my mind was racing for the reason—why me? Why did I happen to be there at that specific moment in time? I was almost pleading with her for a response. Perhaps I was expecting her to soothe my shock and distraught emotional state with a kind word or an explanation of sorts. What happened next is literally out of this world!

This kind and gentle woman looked directly into my eyes; her eyes welled with tears. She began to explain to me about the bags of leaves. She said that those leaves were from her property across the street. The same place where my vehicle was parked was actually in her driveway, where I originally met Victor. She continued to relay to me that for the last several decades, Victor would make his way over to her yard every fall and rake up those leaves. He would then transport them across the street in the large plastic yard bags via his wheelbarrow. He would stuff the leaves between the ground and his house for an insulation barrier. As she wiped away a tear, she said that Victor was like family to her and her children. She said that he was the most blessed man of God she ever knew. She said he read his Bible faithfully every morning and every night. He went to Cross Roads Community Church for the Sunday morning service and the evening service too. He attended the Wednesday night prayer meeting and was also active in his men's church group.

At that moment, everything was beginning to make a little more sense to me. Suddenly, to my surprise, she reached across to me and took hold of both my arms by the wrists. She had her hands around my wrists and lifted my arms a bit so as to draw me nearer to her. I can honestly say I was extremely curious, somewhat nervous, and a little uncomfortable at this gesture by a complete stranger. I stood silent and gazed at her like a child who was about to be taught a valuable lesson. As she held my wrists, she quietly exclaimed, "Now, Joseph, this is going to be a blessing to you!" She went on to explain that over the last several weeks, as she and Victor would gather up the leaves, they would often take a break. During their breaks, she told me they would enjoy a cold beverage like an iced tea or a lemonade and, of course, some good conversation. "Joseph," she went on, "I can't tell you how many times over the last several weeks, during our many conversations, that Victor would convey to me that his greatest fear was that he did not want to have to die alone!"

The tears slipped out of my eyes and down my cheeks. Maybe the emotional buildup of this ordeal

DIVINE INTERVENTION

was finally releasing itself. I thanked Victor's neighbor for sharing that significant bit of the puzzle with me. She went on her way back to her house, and I remained pondering my next move, wiping away tears from my eyes. I headed down the road to the gym, somewhat mesmerized and in mild shock the entire way. The thoughts of my mind spun around in my head like a merry-go-round that I couldn't get off of. I met my workout partner at the gym, and after relaying the story to him, I was hardly in a workout mood, so I headed back home. My wife was surprised to see me back so soon from the gym, and at the same time, she realized I was out of sorts and not myself. I shared my amazing and yet very sad story with her. She comforted me as I shed more tears and attempted to get myself back to some semblance of emotional normalcy.

That fall afternoon, with all of its colorful beauty and drama, stays with me to this day. It turned out that Victor was ninety-one years old and a WWII navy veteran. He apparently didn't have any surviving relatives, save for a distant nephew a few miles away. He did, however, have his neighbor, who might as well have been family to him. They had known each other for better than fifty years! He could confide anything to her, hence even his most intimate thoughts and fears about life and death.

My encounter with Victor A. Kandelin is forever etched in my mind, heart, and soul. Who can call this encounter a chance meeting or a proverbial coincidence? Some would say it was the stars that lined up to bring this event about. Really! After a while, some things just don't look like a coincidence anymore. If I sound redundant, I apologize, but what are the odds! There is no doubt in my mind that Victor was a child of God. God, who loved him to the uttermost, granted Victor the desire of his heart. That deep, heartfelt desire was to not be alone when his time to pass would come. I can only imagine that he would often pray to that end. Can you not see the supernatural power of the Almighty Creator orchestrating even the finest details? I am certain that on that beautiful, late fall day, God was present. On a day when I had my own agenda and my own life to attend to, well, that was not to be the case. God had other plans for me. When the Spirit moves you, it is undeniable! There almost seems to be no way around it. You're going to go, be, and do whatever it takes. The plan will go forward to completion despite your best interests to the contrary, period. I, for one, know exactly what transpired on that late afternoon of Friday, October 23, 2009. I need no convincing. I was called to help facilitate the dying wishes of a child of the King. I stand in awe to know that God can reach down to me, a sinner, and accomplish miraculous and wonderful things. Gosh, who am I but clay in the hands of the master potter! To that end, I say, to God be the glory; great things He has done!

Enough with the Leaves Already!

The time had come to bring our son to college. My wife and I were so excited for him to be able to go off to a university and follow his dreams, while at the same time gaining some higher education and independence. He was on a quest to become a police officer, and so he majored in criminal justice. We set out with our son for the nearly ninety-minute drive. We arrived at the university and soon found ourselves amid the chaos of freshman move-in day. It was late August, and the weather was brutally hot and humid. It was no easy task to move all my kid's belongings up four flights of stairs. After nearly an hour of ascending and descending stairs, I suspect about eight pounds of water weight were shed from my body, and, thanks to God, I managed to avoid a coronary event!

When the move-in was completed, the three of us headed off to a nearby restaurant for lunch. We chatted about how fun and exciting college life was going to be. As a college grad myself, I was able to impart a few of the more important, wisdom-laden dos and don'ts of campus life according to the good book of Dad. "Work hard and then play harder" seems to come to my recollection as a nugget of wisdom I dispensed to him.

During the entire time of the trek to college and throughout the move-in process, I could sense an uneasiness from my son. Later, as we sat for lunch, he had that same quiet, disconnected look on his face. I guess it was just parental intuition—a gut feeling, I suppose. This was his first ever move away from home, and I fully expected the normal amount of homesickness. What new teenage college freshman doesn't experience that on some level, right? My son seemed so withdrawn and disconnected. He just wasn't himself. I shrugged it off and assumed he would get over it and adapt to his new surroundings and the college environment. My hope was that this too would pass. I was hopeful it was just a benign phase he was going through. At this point, only the passage of time will surely tell.

Well, a month had gone by, and the wife and I headed back to the college. It was parent's weekend, and it was all about enjoying each other's company and checking out how your new student was liking the college scene and campus life. We met with our boy, then walked around and toured the campus. Additionally, we were able to meet some of his roommates and newly found friends. After seeing where his classes were and walking around campus, we headed

DIVINE INTERVENTION

to the same nearby restaurant from the previous month on move-in day. Once again, as we sat down to dine, our son didn't seem like his normal self. He was restless and didn't have much to talk about. He was very quiet and restrained. Again, he had that same disconnected, lost look in his eye. Almost like a deer in the headlight look. I probed him a couple of times, asking him if everything was alright. He assured me that he was fine and things were going okay. After eating lunch and spending another half hour or so on campus, with some concern and reservation, the wife and I decided it was time to say goodbye.

We drove the ninety-minute ride home and discussed some concerns over our son's behavior. Our first reaction was that he was probably experiencing some mild depression due to the separation from home. When we arrived home, I opened the back door to the sound of the phone ringing. I rushed in and answered the call, only to hear the voice of my son who we had just left. "What's up, Dude? You miss us already," was my response to him. He replied, in a somewhat concerned tone, if we would come back and get him. He just kept saying he didn't feel well and that he couldn't describe exactly what it was that was bothering him. I remember saying that we had just driven ninety minutes down there, ninety minutes back to home, and now he wanted us to repeat the journey. It was clear something was amiss; he was clearly struggling, and he wasn't going to take no for an answer. He insisted we head back and come get him.

I headed back to the college and found him anxiously awaiting my arrival. Throughout the return drive home, we chatted about what was troubling him. For me, it was a rhetorical question, as I now clearly understood his symptoms to be depression and anxiety. I'm guessing that the separation from home and his very close relationship with his mom and dad were massive triggers. Yet an additional trigger was that he ended up in the hospital for five days during the first week of school due to kidney stones. Good grief! I'm of the impression that the apple doesn't fall far from the tree. I, too, have had to battle this same ugly, hateful anxiety/depression monster on several occasions throughout my life. Now my son, the poor kid, had inherited his old man's gene. A gene I inherited from my mom. I actually felt guilty for what he was suffering through. It's not an easy thing. In my honest opinion, I would rather endure physical pain eight days per week than emotional or mental anguish. I kept reassuring him that he would get through this rough patch; it would just take some time. After spending the weekend at home with the family, I drove him back to college on Sunday night. He had the look of a worried, lost soul when I dropped him off. He was hesitant as he walked back toward his dorm. It seemed like he wanted to come back to the car. My heart was in agony for him, as I knew exactly the torture he was experiencing. I had to let him go and fight for himself. I cried for him on the drive home.

DIVINE INTERVENTION

Over the next few weeks, my son called home many times. I would chat with him and encourage him to go mingle with his college mates, get involved, stay active, and get busy. It seemed as though my words of advice and heartfelt love were futile. They didn't seem to be able to penetrate. Through our many conversations, I could discern that he was becoming hopeless. He didn't appear to be navigating his way out of this newfound scary mindset. His mind and body had learned a new habit and were torturing him. Many more times, I went to retrieve him from college in order to bring him back to the comforts of his own home. I can remember one time at our house, he was pacing and trying to make some sense of how and what exactly he was feeling. He was suffering terribly and paused at the breakfast island. With his hands placed on the counter and his head bowed down, he turned and looked at me. With tears in his eyes, he asked me, "Dad, will I ever be happy again?"

Mind you, up to that point, I never saw him cry, except as a little child, of course. I hugged and cried with him that morning. I will never forget that day. My wife and I were so heartbroken, knowing the anguish he was feeling. As the days and weeks passed, I drove down to the college many times to bring some medication that would curb his anxiety. We would drive around for an hour or so and chat. I did my level best to help him understand how this horrible malady affects a person and how to overcome it. My heart was truly broken knowing what he was experiencing, especially having been there and done that in my own life. I felt helpless to help him. I even read aloud to him a book on how to get out of this malady. Depression is wretched, to say the least! I knew he was suffering. I even suggested that perhaps he take the semester off and come back when he felt better. To my son's credit, he refused that option. I think he knew that if he came home, he wouldn't be going back. His decision to stay in college was extremely admirable! He was so very brave, a warrior and fighter despite the emotional and mental anguish he was enduring. My heart wells up with tears of pride when I consider his will to stay the course and fight the good fight. Oh, dear God, please, I beseech Thee, help my boy!

My son's anguished phone calls continued, and my spur-of-the-moment rescue missions to the college also continued. This routine continued for a couple of months. I worried that he was not going to be able to keep up with his studies and have to drop out. I was continually worried and heartbroken for my son. In fact, I was now beginning to deal with my own anxiety, as I knew exactly what he was feeling. I thought to myself that this sickness is par for the course for a guy my age with all the responsibilities and worries, but for a young kid eighteen years old, no way! My son's health and welfare were continuously on my heart and mind. I would pray several times a day for him to break out of this downward spiral and regain happiness.

DIVINE INTERVENTION

I constantly pray for all my children every day. Often, it's while I'm driving down the road. On one particular beautiful fall day, I was driving along in the neighboring town of Pepperell, Massachusetts. All the while, my son's anxiety and depression were heavy on my heart. I drove by this tiny little ranch house and noticed a very elderly woman hunched over, picking up leaves in her front yard. My best guess was that she was in her late eighties. As usual, my conscience began to kick in, and I was motivated and determined to offer her some help.

I pulled into her driveway while she had her back to me, bending over a pile of leaves. From my rolled-down car window, I said, "Ma'am, could I give you a helping hand with cleaning up the leaves?" Needless to say, she couldn't hear me. I had to yell my offer two more times to get her attention. She finally turned around as I approached her. Her name was Doreen, and she had a British accent and spoke extremely softly. I could barely understand her. It appeared to me that she had possibly endured a stroke at some point, and that hampered her speech and her posture. Her speech was garbled and choppy at best. I had to strain really hard to understand her. At my request to help, she was delighted to let me take over.

I spent the next three hours raking her entire property. She had more leaves on her property than grains of sand on a beach! I must have carried fifteen or twenty tarps to the woods in order to dump them.

The entire time, I was fervently praying for my troubled son. For literally two hours or so, I continually cried out to God to heal my son. I begged Him to give my boy peace and restore him to a normal, happy state. *Please, dear God,* I prayed. *Help my son; help him to be able to enjoy his youth and his college experience.* I carried the tarps and dumped them over and over again. The entire time, I had tears streaming down my face while making known my supplications to God. I can recall saying to God that I wasn't doing these leaves per se for Doreen or for her accolades, but to make God happy. I asked the Lord if He could bless me and my efforts by restoring my son to health and happiness. Over and over, I petitioned God to account my leaf laboring toward my boy and restore him. I even pleaded to put the anxiety and depression on me. I have experienced enduring that type of suffering. I would gladly endure the pain instead of my young son. I must have sounded like a broken record, as my plea was redundant and increasingly desperate. *Please, God,* I prayed. *Please hear my prayer.*

Well, the job was finished. The leaves were all picked up and put in the woods. I folded the tarp and put the rake away as well. All that was left was to say goodbye to Doreen and bid her God bless. I walked up to my newfound, old friend. I told her that the job was all done and that I very much enjoyed meeting her. She thanked me in her choppy, broken, and quivering voice. She was so grateful and repeated over and over to me, "God bless you, God bless you."

DIVINE INTERVENTION

She then perceived to tell me that before I had arrived in her yard, some sort of bird kept chirping my name all morning, Joe, Joe. She said it kept calling again and again. Anyway, I don't recall what kind of bird she said it was. Additionally, I didn't know if that tidbit of information wasn't the mere ramblings of an almost ninety-year-old woman with potentially some cognitive impairment. At any rate, it had me pondering and, if I'm being honest, doubting too. Again, she repeated, "God bless you."

To which I replied, "He always does, and He is so very good to me." I said my last goodbyes and wished her well.

I got into my vehicle and dried my eyes from the tears of my prayers to God and from the emotion of helping this very needy woman. As I drove out the driveway onto the main road, instantly, my cell phone rang. It was my son calling me from college. My heart sank as my worry began to mount. Please, not again! To my sheer amazement, out of the blue, my boy said, "Dad, I feel really, really good! I feel normal again." I feel great was his cry! I was overwhelmed with joy. I questioned him over and over again. He kept reassuring me that he was good, everything was fine, and he felt really good. The anxiety and depression had lifted from him.

"Son, what made the change?" I exclaimed. "What's happened since we last spoke?" To both questions, he had no answer. I expressed how happy I was for him and to go find his friends and have some fun. I encouraged him to enjoy feeling well again and to give thanks to God.

When the call ended, I had no choice but to pull the car over. The tears were literally streaming down my cheeks, and I was sobbing uncontrollably. I was crying tears of relief and tears of gratitude. I was blown away by the thought that my prayer was answered so quickly. How could this be! How did my boy turn on a dime? He went from being afflicted for weeks, even just the day before, to feeling his old self again practically overnight. I was so relieved for him; my joy was bursting. I kept saying, *Really, God! You really answered my cry that fast! Did you really do this?* How can this be! This is crazy! My questioning and doubts slowly morphed into sheer amazement combined with complete and utter gratitude.

I had prayed so fervently that fall day on behalf of my son. I had reached up into the heavens to petition the Almighty to divinely intervene and help us. My heart was bared wide open, and my emotions were pouring out of my eyes in the form of tears. While Doreen sat in the comfort of her home having tea, I labored with leaves, making a plea. God showed me something extremely powerful that fall day. He can do something, anything—literally, in the snap of a finger, in the blink of an eye! He also showed me that he hears the cries of the brokenhearted. I will forever be humbled and eternally grateful for the answer to my groaning, tear-filled prayers that day. I am not saying that God answered my prayers because of my willingness to help out an old lady with her leaves.

DIVINE INTERVENTION

By the same token, I'm not going to dogmatically say that he doesn't either. Let's just say that God knows my heart and its intentions intimately. On that afternoon, I witnessed the awesome power of a loving, caring, and merciful God. In the deepest recesses of my spirit, I knew what had occurred in that moment was supernatural. It was miraculous. It was beautiful! I was blessed, Doreen was blessed, and my son was blessed—the perfect trifecta, like the Father, the Son, and the Holy Spirit. By the way, my son fulfilled his lifetime career desire. He is now a police officer, and he has been so blessed by the Lord, beyond compare. There are no such things as coincidences. No way, no how! Can't you see it? Blessed be the name of the Lord! He is merciful to all who call on Him. He is worthy of honor, praise, glory, and thanks!

My Marine Meets Hanna

My other son was in the United States Marine Corps. Actually, *was* probably isn't the proper word to best describe his military status. The fact is, "Once a marine, always a marine." Ooh rah! At the tender age of eighteen, his MOS (Military Occupational Specialty) was 0311, infantry rifleman. He was a grunt, a hard-charging devil dog! After one year in the corps, he was deployed to a forward operating base (FOB) in Helmond Province, Afghanistan. The marines do seven-month combat deployments. Seven months too long! His mom and I were extremely proud of his decision to join the marine corps. However, as a parent of a deployed marine, we agonized every day, every hour, and every minute of his combat deployment. I don't think a day went by without us praying and crying. After only one month in the country, I had already attended the wake of one of his platoon mates from upstate New York. While in a firefight against an enemy compound, he was killed by a random Taliban bullet. It was devastating! My mind often raced ahead to the thought that this could be my son! Considering how many dangerous night patrols my boy was involved in, I often feared the worst. Every day was an exercise in faith for my wife and me. We fervently pleaded with God to return our son home safe and in good mental, physical, and emotional health. I could go into the many miracles involved during some of his patrol missions, but this chapter is about another, even more obvious, divine intervention.

By the grace of God, our son returned home to us. I will always say that the day he walked over to us upon his arrival home from Afghanistan was far more emotional than the day the doctor handed him to me at his birth. After four years, my son was honorably discharged from the marine corps with the rank of corporal, a noncommissioned officer (NCO). *Semper fidelis*, marine! Thank you for your service to our country. After being home for a few months, he decided to take up the United States Military on their promise of the G.I. Bill. The bill would allow him to receive full tuition and expenses, including living expenses. He would be able to take on any education or career training of his choice at any trade school, college, or university. It's an outstanding, life-altering tool for our well-deserving veterans!

His career choice was to become a helicopter pilot. Gosh! As if being an infantry combat marine wasn't dangerous enough. Apparently, my son doesn't like anything to do with being safe and mundane. He always said that he didn't want a job where he would be miserable for eight hours per day. I should probably be thankful for him wanting to become a helicopter pilot, as he was also considering the option of becoming an underwater welder. I can say one thing about this kid: when he sets his mind to doing something, he goes for it and gets it done. The task involved nearly two years of intensive schooling and pilot training at the University Helicopter Institute in Scottsdale, Arizona. He went on to graduate with a private pilot license, an instrument rating, a commercial rating, a certified flight instructor, and a certified instrument flight instructor. I might also mention he acquired a night vision goggles rating as well.

My son was well on his way up (no pun intended) in his career. To start with, he was flying tours for a company in Tampa Bay. That job is an entry-level position when it comes to the helicopter industry. It's pretty much the starting point for most new pilots. Then my son was miraculously approached by a gentleman from England. He was a national war hero in the Gulf War for the British. His name was James Newton, a.k.a. Mate, and he advanced my son's career by leaps and bounds. Mr. Newton actually has a book published, *Armed Action*. It's all about his helicopter heroics in the Iraq War. It's a fascinating read! That war hero took my son under his wing and put my boy in varying different types of helicopters, doing many different jobs, all the while mentoring him and giving him invaluable life and piloting lessons. I will always be thankful to James Newton for advancing my son's career and life. This newfound friendship was extremely productive.

DIVINE INTERVENTION

It gave my boy oodles of flight time. He accumulated many flight hours, experience, and expertise while flying different choppers.

After working with James for a year or so, my son went to work in the Gulf of Mexico, flying oil rig crews back and forth every two weeks. They call pilots working and living in the Gulf Gomers. After that, he went on to fly medivac flights for Johns Hopkins All Children's Hospital in St. Petersburg, Florida. He left that job because he wasn't getting the flying hours he wanted. He eventually landed (pun intended) back in the Gulf of Mexico, ferrying oil rig crews back and forth to the platforms out at sea. I guess he really enjoyed being a Gomer pilot.

When you fly in the Gulf of Mexico, you most certainly take on some potential risk of losing your life. The weather offshore is entirely unpredictable. The weather can change in an instant due to all the climate factors involved. It is often unpredictable and anybody's guess. On one such day, for my son, it was treacherous and potentially fatal. It was the last few days of July 2020, and Hurricane Hanna was menacing southern Texas. Meanwhile, the spirals, or outer bands of the hurricane, were pushing out toward the east, toward New Orleans, Louisiana. These outer bands of the hurricane were headed toward the flight path of where my son would be flying his helicopter that day to retrieve platform crew workers.

One of the most rigorous courses at the University Helicopter Institute was meteorology. It is an absolute must-learn for pilots. The course is all about the study of atmospheric conditions and how they relate to weather formation. Very early that morning, my son had done his due diligence and researched the necessary information regarding the whereabouts of Hurricane Hanna and her nasty particulars. My boy had done his homework and poured over the graphs, charts, and weather reports. Apparently, the argument from the platform management and the helicopter company management was that the weather was fine out at the rig for the moment. As the pilot in command (PIC), he was advising that the mission be scrubbed for that day. He clearly understood the time involved in getting out to the platform, retrieving crew members, refueling, etc. He further realized that by the time he would be headed in from the field, on his way back to Grand Isle, Louisiana, he could encounter the outer bands of Hurricane Hanna and extreme adverse weather conditions. After making his case to the management on both the platform and to his helicopter company, he decided not to go. However, at the pressure and "gentile persuasion" of both these corporate entities and against his own convictions, as pilot in command, he decided to fly the mission. An educated guess would suggest that perhaps he wanted to please the bosses in spite of more than a gut feeling.

The flight to the platform was approximately one hundred and fifteen miles offshore. It was without incident and took fifty minutes. After his last stop, he was ready to bring a platform employee back to shore. At this point, the wind was howling, and

DIVINE INTERVENTION

my son said he was almost being blown over on the deck. Additionally, the weather was looking ominous and beginning to envelop the entire area. It was a critical moment, in his words. He insisted that if the employee was not in the helicopter in the next few minutes, he would leave without him. He did indeed leave without him. After about thirty minutes of flying and with roughly twenty-five minutes remaining to base, the proverbial junk hit the fan! My boy was being completely overtaken by the horrific weather. A spiral from the hurricane enveloped the entire area of the gulf where he was located. He attempted to go west to avoid what was straight in front of him, but to no avail. He then attempted to go east and try to get around this very ominous weather directly in his flight path home. Running out of options, he turned his ship to head directly through the storm. According to my son, once you "punch in," there is no turning back. He was in full inadvertent IMC flight conditions. IMC stands for instrument meteorological conditions. This is a situation where visibility is less than three miles and the cloud base is less than one thousand feet. The situation my son found himself in was zero visibility and a cloud base at sea level. In this situation, you must be instrument-rated, or you have zero chance of survival!

While the weather in the Gulf of Mexico was tumultuous, my wife and I were in the Gulf of Maine. The weather there was stunning—eighty degrees and pure sunshine. We were sitting on the beach at Short Sands Beach in York, Maine. I love swimming in the ocean, so I made my way into the water. My wife remained behind, lounging in the sun. I waded out into waist-deep water, where I encountered two men. One gentleman was roughly ten years my junior, and the other was about ten years older than me. They were very friendly toward me, so we engaged in conversation. The topic of how crazy the world was becoming was injected into our conversation. Oftentimes, I find a way to introduce myself as a Christian and present a biblical perspective as to the hows and whys of why the world seems to be spinning around the drain. I would say that for the better part of half an hour, I was preaching the gospel of Jesus Christ. Both of these men were of a particular denomination that comes from Rome.

I did my best to keep the conversation on the topic of a "relationship" with God versus a "religion," on a gospel of grace versus a system of man-made works and religiosity. I was attempting to point out the difference between the capital r and the small r, if you catch my meaning. They both asked me profound questions concerning my beliefs. I answered them with a biblical response, not an opinion. I must say they were very humble, openly inquisitive, and accepting of my mini sermon on the water. I could sense they were somewhat moved by the good news that was being preached. They thanked me for sharing with them, and they claimed they were genuinely and sincerely glad for our chance meeting and what they now had to ponder about. I guess the gift of evangelism that God has given me doesn't take a

DIVINE INTERVENTION

vacation, not even on a beautiful Maine beach. I'm not complaining. It's a most wonderful gift and a calling I try to stay true to.

I walked out of the water and back to my loving, ever-patient, and understanding wife. She gets it, and she is a saint when it comes to waiting on me sometimes. There will be rewards waiting for her when she meets her Savior, that I'm sure of. When I got back to my beach chair, I sat down, and my cell phone rang. It was my helicopter pilot son.

My son is an instrument-rated pilot. He turned directly northeast into the storm to head for base. All the while, he had no autopilot in that ship or radar, and he lost communications with the base. He even lost GPS for a time. It's the same GPS we use on our cell phones or in our cars. Obviously, it's a bit more detailed and sophisticated. He had his cell phone, which, amazingly enough, had a signal. Eventually, his GPS came on line. My boy was being thrown about the cockpit—up and down, left and right. It was violent, according to his words. It was akin to riding a bucking bronco. Meanwhile, back at the base, the company has a system called FlightAware. It is a sophisticated tracking system that knows a pilot's exact position and literally every move he's making. My son was flying in fifty-miles-per-hour winds. He was in a deluge of torrential rain; there were no wipers on the helicopter, and the thunder and lightning were awe-inspiring. Although there was no awe to be had, there was only pure, unadulterated fear.

My son made a call to the helicopter base in order to speak with the chief pilot, Sean. Sean has spent more than thirty years flying in the gulf. Initially, my boy told me that he had my cell number ready to dial. He wanted to tell us that he loved us and that he wasn't going to make it. On second thought, he realized he didn't want us to hear him as he fell to his demise in the tumultuous sea below. Sean took the call from my son only to hear a frightened young pilot say, "I'm not going to make it!"

"Don't say that! You need to take a couple deep breaths and focus on the task," was the chief pilot's response. He told my son that the entire staff was watching him on the FlightAware system. Sean told him to steer a specific heading and do his absolute best to keep the ship straight and level. "You can do this; we're all pulling for you and praying." My son dropped down to a hard deck he set for himself, one hundred feet off the waves. He explained to me that if pilots go below one hundred feet, they don't usually make it back alive. His idea was that, at one hundred feet, perhaps he could get a visual of the sea below through his chin bubble. The chin bubbles are the glass windows at his foot controls. However, even at one hundred feet above the ocean, he had zero visibility. He flew his butt off for nearly twenty minutes solely with handheld controls and by scanning only instrument gauges for flight and navigation. A ferocious outer spiral of Hurricane Hanna was inflicting her best on my son's helicopter. He was fighting for his life!

DIVINE INTERVENTION

After twenty minutes of sheer hell, my son was out of the worst of it. He was able to see through thick haze, some land through his chin bubble, and head for base. After landing the ship, his hands and feet were numb, his flight suit was completely soaked from sweat, and he was sick to his stomach. The chief pilot, Sean, was waiting for him, as well as the office personnel. My son, in a tirade, proceeded to use coarse language to explain to the chief pilot that he told them in the morning that the mission wasn't going to be safe. He screamed to him that this will *never* happen again as he is the pilot in command (PIC), and his decision to go or stay is the final word and authority. At that point, the chief pilot embraced my boy with compassion and responded, "I know, son." They had a brief cry together and realized just how close they came to what may have been a tragedy.

On the beach in Maine, as my son relayed this horrifying event to me, I was reduced to tears and sobbing hard. I had to put a beach towel over my head, as I did not want any of the surrounding beachgoers to see me in this condition. What broke me even more was when my son told me he was one hundred times more afraid during that hellacious flight than any of the horrors he personally experienced in the war in Afghanistan. He was convinced he was going to die in the sea. My boy and I sobbed together and gave thanks to God that he survived.

After we both had our cries, I asked him, When precisely did this event take place? What was the exact time he was enduring these twenty-three minutes of horror? He claimed that it had just happened in the last hour; he had just arrived back at base. I could not contain my mix of excitement and emotion as I told him of my sermon while wading in the ocean over the last hour. At the same time, my son flew that helicopter through the storm, and I was expounding on the grace and mercy God demonstrated on the cross. My heart was full of love and sincerity as I poured out the message of His Son while wading waist-deep in the sea. In the meantime, God Almighty dispatched his angels that morning to surround my son in his cockpit and deliver him safely back to his base. While I was in the sea, enjoying the ocean and good company, my son was over the sea in God's hands. By the way, no more than ten minutes after my boy landed at the base in Grand Isle, it became completely enveloped by the storm. Landing blind in those conditions would have taken a miracle. However, the miracle had already taken place in those twenty minutes passing through the hell of Hurricane Hanna's outer spiral. Who can deny that our Creator isn't present in times of need? I am convinced God honored my faithfulness that morning while I was preaching and expounding His Word while wading in the sea. Simultaneously, in His love and mercy, He was keeping my son out of the sea! To God be given all the glory and all the thanks and praise. Thank You, Father, for the beauty of the sea. Thank You, God, for saving my son. Thank You for saving my marine!

DIVINE INTERVENTION

Thank You for saving us eternally by Your Son so that one day we will stand together by the crystal sea! Thank You, Jesus!

A Daughter's Intuition

Most families experience some dysfunction at various levels. What's worse is when you add some ethnicity to the mix. In my family, we have both Italian and Portuguese heritage. That European combo is akin to mixing fire and gasoline together. Additionally, growing up in a large family—five brothers and one sister—can also lend itself to some very tumultuous situations. Oftentimes, varying individual values, morals, and personalities can, regrettably, get in the way of any lasting peace among siblings. It's unfortunate, but keeping up amicable relationships and remaining civil to one another can, on many occasions, be something to grasp at. Unfortunately, this is a stark reality for many families—a reality to which my family is no exception.

I want to be careful not to disparage or demonize family members in the process of relating this particular testimony. Suffice it to say, I have a very strenuous relationship with one particular sibling. I question if there was ever a meaningful relationship at all. On numerous different occasions, we have had

DIVINE INTERVENTION

tremendous fallings-out. Falling-outs, of which there seems to be no point of return! However, time and time again, I have ceded my own wants, needs, desires, and perhaps even my ego to make an attempt at yet another lasting truce. This was often an extremely difficult thing to do. Over and over, I would surrender my will to the greater and higher cause. All the while, my conscience would be reminding me, convicting me, of a great verse of scripture: "To whom much is given much will be required" (Luke 12:48). In my heart of hearts and to the core of my being, I count myself as someone to whom much has been given, namely the gift of salvation and eternal life! I would have to be willfully blind to ignore that overwhelming truth. The blessings I have received are innumerable and immeasurable. These last few chapters of my life's testimonies most definitely attest to that readily apparent fact! Moreover, these testimonials are but a small glimpse of the divine blessings afforded me throughout my entire life thus far.

Forgive me if I sound too cliché, but I think every man has his breaking point! The latest sibling infraction thrust upon me was the one that broke the camel's back. It was the hill to die on and make my stand. Pardon all the clichés; they do, however, make the intended point. The latest volley of our sibling rivalry wound up involving my father. At the time, he was ninety! Regrettably, more than likely, due to his advanced age and at the suggestion of my sibling, my dad had been made a party to something that was very egregious toward me and my marine son. My son is a hero to me; he served in combat in Helmond Province, Afghanistan, for seven months. He was deployed with the Third Battalion, Ninth Marine Division, at a forward operating base. Wherein this latest nonsensical infraction by my sibling involved not just me but my hero son, it put me over the edge.

It would be best to spare all the dramatic details. The reality of the matter is that it had a tremendous negative impact on me emotionally. My spirit was crushed! It was at this last straw that I decided to toss in the towel. I would sever ties entirely with my dad and my sibling. I had gone back too many times and had no more forgiveness left in the tank. The forgiveness well had run dry. What remained was extreme hurt, bitterness, disappointment, anger, frustration, despair, and, most of all, hopelessness at having any meaningful or lasting relationships. At this point, top of mind was self-preservation. I would never again allow this toxicity into my life, a toxicity that stems from the full-blown manifestation of man's pride. Having seen and experienced this malady firsthand and for years, I counted the cost and remained firm in my decision to avoid that sibling and my dad at all costs! I was determined to stay my course and stay away. Nothing would deter me! In my mind, it was clear. Unfortunately, I knew that I would never see my dad again.

The years dragged by slowly—four to be exact! My dad was now ninety-four. The four years without him were very painful. On many occasions, I wrestled with the notion of a truce with my dad. I believe

DIVINE INTERVENTION

God's Spirit has nudged me many times to seek out my father. The Spirit showed me in many different ways that I needed to go see my father. However, in my hurt, pain, and self-preservation mode, I would resist the idea of reconciliation. This was also, in large part, due to the conflict of being around that sibling as well.

Over the years, I have heard many a pastor preach on the subject of forgiveness and reconciliation. I had even sought out advice and counsel, seeking to determine what my options were. However, there wasn't anybody or anything that could convince me to seek out my dad. Alas, I was so broken in spirit that resolution seemed light-years away and perhaps even futile. I had to avoid, with all the strength I could muster, any notion of reconciliation. I was resolute in my conviction. It would take no less than a massive miracle for me to come around. Thankfully, God is in the business of miracles.

Ask, and you shall receive! Miracles come at diverse times and in diverse places. I was lying awake one evening in bed with much on my mind. Thoughts of my aging father and how much time he had remaining on this earth were swimming in the clutter of my restless and sleepless brain.

At 1:09 a.m., my cell phone lit up and buzzed with an incoming text message. I was surprised and worried at the same time. My twenty-four-year-old daughter would be driving home from her waitressing job at this hour. As I looked on my phone, I observed that the text was indeed from my daughter.

After my initial panic, I realized she sent me a link to an audio recording. Her message simply read, "Dad, I listened to this audio; it's really good, and I immediately thought of you. I feel like God put it on my heart to give it to you. Anyway, take a listen; I hope it helps you."

Well, I took her advice, and in that moment, I clicked on the link. On the audio recording, there were three Christian gentlemen discussing the concept of forgiveness. My initial thought was, *Oh great, here we go again, same old, same old!* My initial instinct was to click the link close and resume my ongoing battle, attempting to find that peaceful, restful slumber. However, that was not to be the case. My night was about to be radically transformed. I knew I would have to give an account to my daughter, whether I listened to the audio or not. So partly to please my daughter, Olivia, and to satisfy a little curiosity, I dared to listen. I listened for a moment, and that moment turned into a minute, and that minute became the entire duration of the audio.

The three men had something in their voices that was so genuine, so caring, so true, and laden with Christlike humility. I could literally feel their love and emotions. They shared and exchanged thoughts and ideas on the subject of true forgiveness and what that looks like practically. I had never heard such a heartbreaking truth. Perhaps in the past, I didn't want to; maybe I wasn't ready to hear it. As I listened on, I was being completely and utterly broken. My spirit was crushed within me. Remorse and

DIVINE INTERVENTION

sorrow don't begin to describe my emotional state at that early hour of the morning. I found myself weeping and sobbing uncontrollably. I was a basket case; my sobbing awoke my wife. She asked me what the matter was; I looked at her, tears streaming down my face, and simply said, "I must go see my dad!"

Within a couple of days, amid much angst and prayer, I worked up the courage to go visit my dad, fourteen miles down the road. I arrived and knocked on his front door several times, as he doesn't hear well and is nearly fully blind. It took him a few minutes to open the door; he has very limited mobility as well. I greeted him with a louder than normal, "Hi, Dad!" However, because of his blindness and failing faculties, he didn't quite know who I was. With a second effort, I greeted him again and announced my name; he was overjoyed. We hugged and cried at the front door. He was saying how glad he was to see me, and he kept asking me where I had been. I assisted him into the house by holding onto his arm and walking, leading him down the hallway to his television room.

We chatted for a long while. Inevitably, the question of where I had been came up again. I explained to him what had transpired that brought so much hurt to me and why I decided to stay away for the last four years. It seemed that he barely remembered the circumstances, if he remembered them at all. My dad was genuinely sorry, and the look of remorse on his face was very telling. He kept muttering *tsk, tsk,* and moving his head back and forth, as if he were ashamed, as I relayed my side of the story. He was

123

crushed! We cried again, and he apologized for hurting me and would repeat that he never meant to do that to me. The longer I stayed and conversed with my dad, I knew his mind was failing and he was experiencing dementia, or Alzheimer's. It was becoming very clear to me that there were periods of complete lucidness mingled with confusion, total memory loss, and repetitious questions. I was amazed at the difference in him that occurred over the four-year period. After chatting for a couple of hours, we made our way to the door and said our goodbyes with hugs and kisses. Just before I was leaving, my dad looked at me and asked me why I had been away. I was overwhelmed with the reality of his condition and what I had missed. I responded that it was okay, Dad; we didn't need to talk about it. He insisted that I tell him. He had completely forgotten all about our conversation moments earlier in his television room.

As I drove away in the car, I was moved to tears and sobbed profoundly, in part because I had allowed four years to pass and my dad's health had certainly and notably declined. I was also crying in large part because I was going to get a second chance at loving my dad again. Over the next few months, my father and I had some great times together when I visited. We would go out to lunch and take scenic rides in the car. We had great fellowship talking about memories and life. I would bring him back to my house for dinner and dessert. On the fourteen-mile drive back to his house, we would sing Frank Sinatra, Dean Martin, and Englebert Humperdinck songs. It was so

DIVINE INTERVENTION

hilarious as well because dad wanted to know who I was talking to when I would instruct Siri to play these musical artists. "Who are you talking to? Who is Siri, Joe?" He cracked me up! When we arrived back at his house, he would always thank me and say he had a great time and really enjoyed himself. "Be sure to thank Pam for dinner," would be his parting words as I would lead him in through the front door.

Before long, Dad had some health issues, including some congestive heart failure and even some delirium. The latter, I wouldn't wish on anyone! He was in the hospital for a week and then moved to a rehab facility for a couple of weeks. I would visit him often, and during my visit, I would actually feed him his meals. It was tough for him to feed himself because of his blindness. "You're a great feeder, Joe," he would say, and we would have a good chuckle about that. I felt like a mother bird when she fed her chicks and they opened their beaks wide. It was like feeding my children when they were babies. I so enjoyed feeding my dad and was honored to do for him what he did for me as a child. Dad went home to live with my sibling, with whom I would have no contact. As a result, I saw him few and far between. On one such occasion, my wife and son arranged to pick him up on my sixtieth birthday. They completely surprised me. In fact, my wife made up the ruse that I had to be home at noon to wait for the arrival of a UPS package. I came to my back door only to be greeted by my dad, with my wife and my police officer son holding him on either side, walking up the walkway.

It was glorious! I was overwhelmed, and it brought tears to my eyes. I exclaimed in a choked-up voice, "Dad, I'm sixty years old today!" We hugged among quiet tears.

I often think about what my life would have been like had my daughter not sent me that audio recording at 1:09 a.m. It was obviously weighing heavily on her heart that her dad didn't have a relationship with his dad, her grandfather. The Holy Spirit put it on her heart to send me a balm that could heal the wound—a wound so deep that only a supernatural balm would suffice—a balm that could penetrate even the most hardened heart. Let's recall: I was determined to stay away from my dad. However, my Dad in heaven had a different plan for His kid. God used "my kid" to reach out to me, "His kid," so my dad could once again see "his kid" before he departs this world. That's how God does things! That late night, as I lied awake, God used the wisdom-laden, graceful conversation of those three godly Christian men—just sharing their thoughts on what forgiveness looks like and how to flesh it out. Their Spirit-filled words penetrated the Spirit in me. I was completely broken and humbled to the core. That audio recording was the impetus to set me on the road to forgiveness and rekindling a relationship with my dad, a relationship that had been severed four long years prior. My daughter yielded to the Holy Spirit and sent me the healing balm.

God orchestrated the entire affair. He loves me with such love that He reached out to me. My Father

DIVINE INTERVENTION

in heaven desired for me to forgive and love my father on earth. He did not want me to live with the emotional pain that comes from remorse and regret when the time comes for my dad to go home to our heavenly Father. At my dad's age of ninety-four, perhaps God broke me for all the right reasons in the eleventh hour of Dad's life. God didn't want me to carry that pain for the rest of the days of my life, nor did He want my dad to be without his son reconciled to him before his time would come to die. Once again, God has clearly woven His divine will into the fabric of my life. His divine intervention has brought about peace, love, healing, and restoration. Who would have thought that a daughter's intuition and a text message at 1:09 a.m. could bring about such a blessed outcome? God knew! His love works in mysterious ways and at diverse times and places. All things are possible with God. I am so thankful that God was patient with me and persevered after me to achieve the desired outcome so that all could be the benefactors of His divine grace! To Him be given all the thanks, all the praise, and all the glory! I love you, Olivia! I love you, Dad! Most of all, I love you, Father, Son, and Holy Spirit!

As an afterthought, I have forgiven my sibling as well, and that relationship has been restored. My dad passed away four days shy of the age of ninety-five. I was able to see him alone one day at the hospital. By God's grace, he was lucid, fully alert, and talkative, as opposed to the previous day, where heavy sedation for pain kept him asleep. It was amazing! You would never believe he only had a few days remaining. I was able to witness the rally a person often gets when very near death. That time we had together was entirely a gift from our heavenly Father. I believe it was a reward for reconciling with my dad. It was a serendipitous closure for both of us. I will never forget it! My only regret is that I wish I had stayed longer to chat that day in the hospital. That day was the last time I would see my dad. He went home to my sibling's house, and within a week, Dad went home to be with the Lord. I am convinced that Dad would have been very happy to know I reconciled with my sibling. I know my heavenly Father is happy as well.

Ivy on the Beach

For as long as I can remember, the ocean has always been my favorite place to be. Way back in my childhood, my dad would bring us to the sea and places in Massachusetts called Salem Willows, Pioneer Village, and Castle Island. My memories of the smell of the ocean air, swimming in saltwater, seagulls chirping, and beautiful sandy beaches are irreplaceable. As a young boy, I had so much enjoyment at the ocean. Being with my family, playing with my siblings, and bathing in the warm sunshine was such a joy. When I look at the ocean today, I marvel at how vast it is. Its boundaries appear limitless; her horizons seem to have no end. It truly is a glorious part of this creation and formally declares the magnificent handiwork of our Creator!

Just recently, on a particularly warm early June day, my wife and I set out for the beach. It wasn't an ordinary spring day. The temperature was at least ten degrees above the normal seventy degrees for that time of year. It was also a day without clouds and full, bright sunshine. We gathered our beach amenities—

cooler, umbrella, chairs, sunscreen, and, of course, snacks—and made our way to Hampton Beach, New Hampshire. We arrived at low tide, my favorite time, and decided to take a long walk down to the south toward the state park. It was an incredible beach day—literally, a perfect ten!

As we made our way back from walking to the jetty, I noticed a woman acting frantically. She was talking to another woman; her hands were waving about, and she appeared hysterical. As Pam and I made our way over to question the commotion, she made her way off at a rapid pace. It seemed like she was running in a state of confusion to-and-fro. My curiosity was getting the best of me, so we approached the woman she was talking to. I inquired as to what's going on. The woman told us that the lady had lost her little daughter. I asked the woman for her age, description, and how long she had been missing. Her responses were heartbreaking. The little girl was five years old; she was wearing a blue bathing suit, had blond curly hair, and was a tad chubby. Oddly enough, I forgot to ask the woman what the child's name was. Go figure! She had been missing for forty-five minutes! Is it any wonder that her mother was frantically scouring the beach in a full-blown panic state? Dear God!

Pam and I were distraught with that terrible sinking feeling in our stomachs. As parents of four children, we can somewhat only imagine what that woman was experiencing. We lost our oldest for about ten minutes when he was around age three.

DIVINE INTERVENTION

He wandered away in less than thirty seconds of me being distracted. One second, he was at the swing set, and a few short seconds later, he was gone. I can personally attest to the fact that there is no sicker feeling than what runs through your thoughts when your child is missing. Fortunately, we retrieved him within ten minutes or so. However, those were probably ten of the most agonizing minutes of my life! Fortunately, he didn't stray very far. The joy we felt when he was located was indescribable. This poor woman at the beach was missing her little girl for forty-five minutes!

Pam and I started walking back to our beach chairs. I began constantly scanning the beach, both up on the sand and along the low-tide waterfront. The volume of people at the beach that day was crazy! The entire beach was slammed with people as far as the eye could see in all directions. Hampton Beach is over one and a half miles long, north to south. It seemed more like a mid-August day than an early June day. Beach umbrellas dotted the landscape, appearing as if a giant, multicolored canopy stretched end to end. I looked to my wife, and I remember uttering doom-filled phrases with a near hopeless tone in my voice. With an anxious reservation, I was saying, "This is futile; there is no way you can find anyone in this crowd!" This is like searching for a needle in a haystack! That sinking, anxious feeling in my gut was growing stronger and bringing on nausea.

As we continued to walk back to our spot on the beach, another fifteen minutes had passed by.

Throughout the walk back, I was praying—more like begging—God to have this young girl found. I specifically prayed, *Dear God in heaven, please let me find this little girl! Please, God, help me find her!* Over and over, that was my mantra. If not me, then please let someone find this child.

We had just arrived back at our chairs, cooler, and umbrella. I took a last intense gaze up at the sand and a final look down toward the water. I was scanning left to right on the beach uncovered by the receding tide. The ocean was directly in front of me, and there were hordes of beachgoers everywhere. All of a sudden, approximately one hundred yards ahead of me—quite a distance, I might add—I spy a little girl. I was straining to see that far, but she was walking from the north to the south, from my left to my right, and she was all alone. I'm somewhat color-blind, so I immediately grabbed hold of my wife and directed her to gaze down toward the water. I couldn't get the words out of my mouth fast enough! "Is that a blue bathing suit? She is walking alone, right? Hun, I think that might be the lost girl! Quick, let's go!" I exclaimed with excited anticipation.

We ran as fast as our legs would carry us toward the child. As I was within ten feet of the little girl, I signaled for a lifeguard to come over my way. I approached this little girl with the blond curly hair and blue bathing suit, hoping and praying that I hit the jackpot! I said, "Hi, honey, are you lost?" With tears streaming down her face and nodding her head up and down, she said yes. The lifeguard then asked

DIVINE INTERVENTION

her if her name was Ivy. Again, with tears streaming down her beautiful little face, she replied yes.

The lifeguard then looked at me and said, "Good eye, dude!"

I picked her up in my arms; she was sobbing and said, "I only wanted to show them this shell!"

As she held out the shell, I told her, "My name is Joe, and this is my wife, Pam." I went on to say, "Mr. Lifeguard, what is your name?" He said his name was Jack. I explained, "Ivy, this is Jack, and he is going to help us. Ivy, honey, you are not lost anymore! We found you! It's going to be okay, Ivy. Jack is calling your mommy on that phone thing he's holding. She is coming to get you right now!" I think in that moment, I felt Ivy squeeze me just a little tighter as she sobbed a tad quieter.

I can only imagine the absolute, sheer relief Ivy's mom must have felt when she heard Jack's voice over another lifeguard's radio saying, "We have the child!" At this point, Ivy was missing for over an hour!

I was looking off in the distance with excited anticipation, awaiting the arrival of Ivy's mother. All the while, I kept assuring little Ivy that her mommy was coming soon.

In the distance, I viewed three people running through the hot, dry sand on the upper beach. It was Ivy's mom and two sisters, about seven and eight years old. I set Ivy down on the sand as her family was arriving. The reunion of the mom and her three daughters is something I will never forget. The mom got down on one knee and embraced all three girls within the circumference of her outstretched arms. They were all crying and sobbing almost hysterically. Ivy's sisters kept repeating over and over again, "Oh, Ivy. Oh, Ivy!" The scene had me in quiet tears. Emotionally, I was a basket case and was holding back the full onslaught of my emotions. I didn't want to create another scene, I suppose.

My heart was so filled with joy as I watched this incredibly emotional reunion with both my wife and Jack, the lifeguard, at my side. We were all so thankful and overjoyed at this wonderful outcome. As I was cherishing that very joyous moment, Ivy's mom looked up at me. Her expression of gratitude was written all over her face. She reached out her arm toward me from the huddle she was in with her girls. She extended her hand, signaling for me to put my hand forth toward hers. She clasped my hand and was squeezing it with tears streaming down her face. It was overwhelming! She looked straight into my eyes and repeatedly said, Thank you, thank you! I responded to her by saying that God did this. I told her about my prayer, begging God to let me find her daughter. I explained that just moments after asking Him, God put her squarely in my line of sight. I repeated that I didn't do this; God did. I was as sincere as a person can be when my eyes met hers, and I said, "To God be the glory! Give Him the thanks and praise. He did this!" She was emotionally overwhelmed and looked directly up toward the heavens and kept repeating thank You, thank You. At that moment, Pam and I made our way back to our beach

DIVINE INTERVENTION

chairs. With a friendly wave of goodbye and a smile from ear to ear that you couldn't wipe away from our jubilant faces, we were gone.

What an *amazing* experience! How can I explain it any other way? Coincidence? I think not! Luck? No way! There is not an inkling of doubt in my mind that God responded and answered my prayer and Ivy's mother's prayer that day. If you had been a witness to the masses of humanity on Hampton Beach that afternoon, then you could fully appreciate this stunning miracle. I am at times recalling this event and am somewhat in disbelief. Did this really happen? Of all the thousands of beachgoers there that day, what are the odds it would be me to spot Ivy walking down the beach! It would appear that I often find myself in these types of situations. The previous chapters decry this fact. Why me? Who am I? I'm certainly no saint! However, I do know this one thing: that day, my heart was so burdened for this little lost five-year-old. I begged my Lord to let me find her, and He answered my cry. God is real; He is awesome, and He most definitely hears the cries of His people. I am honored and humbled to be called by God to be a vessel in various times and places. God knows the attitude of my heart; He knows my innermost thoughts. His Spirit lives in me. I always stand at the ready, and I'm willing and able to answer the call for His glory and praise. Here I am, God, send me! Thank You, heavenly Father, for answering my prayer. Thank You, dear God, for steering me in the direction of little Ivy on the beach!

One Step One Second

love to keep my property as neat and meticulous as I can. Every couple of years, I resurface the driveway with five-gallon buckets of tar sealer. Every spring, I power wash the siding on the house, wash the windows, clean out the sheds, and on and on it goes. My favorite and ultimate property task is to keep and maintain my beautiful lawn. I like to have it look like a lawn in *Better Homes & Garden* magazine. It's my showpiece. What can I say? It's sort of an obsession. Despite the labor involved, it gives me satisfaction and relaxes me when I water it and enjoy its deep green beauty. The lawn is most definitely a lot of work! It requires multiple different fertilizers, overseeding, lime, grub control, insect control, and even fungus control as well. It can get expensive! I figured you get out of the lawn what you put into it. I pour tender love, care, and money into it. Oh, I forgot to mention water! Water costs money too. It just never seems to end. It's most definitely a luxury expense.

On one particular beautiful day in June, I set out to cut the lawn and weed-whack the entire prop-

DIVINE INTERVENTION

erty. As is customary, since I moved in many years ago, I haul my grass clippings across the main road, which is a major route—Route 119, to be specific. I really don't have a proper place or the space to put them on my property, so across the street into the woods they go. I spread them out in a particular area, and they mulched down quite nicely. Between the fall leaves and the summer grass clippings, I often make several trips across the main road throughout the year. It's a moderately traveled road with a decent amount of traffic. One definitely needs to take care when crossing. As our parents often exclaimed when we were kids, don't forget to look both ways!

The entire time I was working that afternoon, my Bose headphones were blasting my favorite songs into my ears. After about two or three hours, the job was finished, and it came time to haul the grass clippings across the main road. I grabbed the full barrel and was toting it along behind me. I walked up to Main Street, and while enjoying the song "Sweet Child o' Mine" by the group Guns N' Roses, I looked in both directions. I looked to my right toward the west, and there were no vehicles in sight whatsoever. I then looked to my left, toward the east, and saw a pickup truck at least two hundred yards away. I had enough time to go back and forth across the road three times if I wanted to. There was more than sufficient time to make a safe crossing with my grass clippings in tow.

I made exactly one step onto the main road, 119, all the while enjoying the song playing in my ears. My full attention was focused straight ahead of me in the woods across the street. In that precise *instant*, a motorcycle traveling approximately fifty to sixty miles per hour screamed by me at no more than twelve inches from my face. The rider, in a full-face helmet, turned to his right to look squarely into my eyes. His gaze was laden with shock, fear, and surprise. His eyes were bugged out, wide open! The look on his face was one of sheer terror. I was stopped dead in my tracks and was trying to understand what just happened. I stood there in horror and utter disbelief! I could not have been caught off guard anymore. Now, when I say he was a foot away, I might be exaggerating a bit; it was probably less! The motion and speed of the passing motorcycle literally took my breath away for a second, and I gasped.

I *never* saw the motorcycle! I only saw a pickup truck far off in the distance. In my mind, everything was good to go. *Wrong!* To this day, I don't know if the rider passed that pickup truck or if I just completely missed seeing him. I guess it's irrelevant. If that motorcycle hit me at that speed, I would have been killed instantly—mangled! I'm certain that the motorcycle rider would have been killed as well. What's important to realize is that I didn't react to the motorcycle as if to jump back and get out of the way. I simply walked into the road without any expectation of a vehicle in my path. The speeding bike just passed me—literally, met me—at the exact same instant I stepped out. Perhaps if the headphones weren't on my head, I may have heard the motorcycle approaching.

Throughout the rest of that day, my mind kept racing with thoughts of what-if scenarios. I literally kept having visions play out in my mind's eye of what could have been. Every vision that my imagination would conjure up was horrifying—quite gory, in fact. I kept having to pause and experience these thoughts. They would just wash over me. My anxiety was rising, and the tears would begin to well up. I think I was experiencing some shock. I kept thinking about what my wife would have seen; she was in the house, just a few feet away. My thoughts kept bringing me back to the events that could have unfurled in the days ahead for my wife and children. A closed casket funeral was among those disturbing visions. I was in the grip of my own imagination and had to keep shrugging those horrifying thoughts away. It's as if I were in a repeating loop, like a record that is scratched and playing over and over. In retrospect, I suppose that perhaps this is the result of a traumatic event. What I was experiencing was probably normal in this situation. At least a few times that day, I had to seek out my wife and talk it out with her. I attempted to explain what I was feeling. I desperately needed to let it go and be reassured that everything was alright. I was trying really hard to comprehend what had happened, attempting to understand this overwhelming and untimely debacle.

There is a saying that timing is everything. In this scenario, that's an understatement. Timing was a matter of life and death! I am convinced that, as humans, we live in the here and now. Our existence is temporal. Our Creator, however, lives in the eternal. Yesterday, today, and the future of all our tomorrows are all in the *now* for God. He is sovereign and in total control. He is present everywhere and at all times. I'm convinced that God presided over the events of that fateful afternoon. When I think about the miniscule events leading up to my standing at the edge of the road, I can go crazy pondering the details. What if I was just a little slower, dragging the bucket along, or a little faster? What if I gazed a little longer, looking east and west? It comes down to no more than a second, perhaps even a half-second. A second in this scenario makes all the difference—the difference between life and death. It comes down to one second and one step, or less!

Do I sound redundant when I say that it wasn't my time, nor was it my day? If left to my own timing and planning, I'd be dead and buried, and my wife would be widowed! On that beautiful summer afternoon, God's plan was to keep me around for a while longer. Perhaps angels were dispatched to hold me off for a split second while picking up the grass clippings or while walking up to the main road. Maybe the motorcycle rider was delayed one second longer or sped up by one second. Everything aligned in such a way that as I stepped onto the main road, I was within one second and one step away from certain, instant death. Isn't it ironic that the tune playing in my headphones as I stepped into an almost certain

DIVINE INTERVENTION

death was "Sweet Child o' Mine" by Guns N' Roses? I'm not a big fan of them; it just happened to be on my playlist. Coincidence? Not a chance! I am His, and He is mine! I'm certain of it. I am so far beyond thankful, so utterly humbled, and amazed at the grace and mercy of God. He has spared me yet again! Oh, God, to what end? Why? What do You still have for me to do? I am curious and speechless as to Your plan for me. Thank You for sparing me. Thank You for Your watchful eye. Thank You for allowing me to remain with my wife and kids until the day You decide to call me home. Your will be done, Father.

My Personal Testimony of Salvation

You may recall chapter 10 of this book entitled, "Take Me Out to the Ball Game." In that chapter, I shared the story of my mom's passing. The numerous uncanny circumstances and the timing of those events surrounding that day were all under the watchful eye of Almighty God. I'm certain that everything I had seen and experienced throughout those very sad days was divinely allowed and was directly responsible for leading me to a saving knowledge of Jesus Christ. I am also certain that none of it was a coincidence. I often say that watching my mom pass away was a very traumatic and extremely unfortunate event in my life. It is a memory I will take with me to my grave! It was, however, the single most fortuitous event of my life. It humbled me to my core. It broke me and was 100 percent responsible for my journey to search out and understand the true living God. Like in *The Blues Brothers*, Dan Aykroyd and John Belushi were known to say in the movie, "We're on a

DIVINE INTERVENTION

mission from God," so, too, was I now on a mission, given from God to find out God.

My mom died on Thursday, February 27, 1992, at around three thirty in the afternoon in the bedroom of her home in Groton, Massachusetts. Again, it was one day after she came home from the hospital. So much for the doctor's opinion of my mom living "another fourteen days, at least a minimum of ten" after being sent home from the hospital. I was summoned, via a phone call, to my parents' house by my oldest brother. His voice was calm but also laden with urgency. "Get here quickly," he said. "Please don't speed. Be careful, but, Joe, get here!"

I never did obey his caution about speeding. I arrived at my parents' home, the same home I grew up in. I proceeded down the hallway to their bedroom on the right. As I turned into my mom's bedroom, I beheld a horrifying sight. It took me completely off guard. I thought I had seen everything that this vicious, diabolical cancer could manifest up to this point. However, I was not prepared for what it looked like to watch a human being about to expire, let alone your own mom. Those last two or three hours in my mom's bedroom, I watched in anguish as her life was slowly and methodically ebbing away. Her physical body was shutting down system by system. I know now, after some later research I did, that it was a physical, anatomical, and necessary process. However, at the time, in my mind, it seemed so undignified and cruel. It was as though this was some sort of spectacle, like she was on public display for all the world to behold at her worst hour. My mom lied there, perishing from this plane of existence, and there was nothing I could do about it. I was helpless, hopeless, and emotionally drained. The whole scene horrified me! It terrified me! I was the first person, among my entire family members in the room, to say out loud that my mom had taken her last breath.

As I glanced over at the hospice lady, she had a tear running down her cheek; she nodded a solemn yes to me. Why is she crying? She does this for a living! She should be used to this horrifying scene. Oddly enough, the word she used was "serendipitous." *What!* I didn't understand. I was angry! Actually, way beyond angry. To the depths of my being, I was overflowing with pure, unadulterated rage! Serendipitous! That was the last word on my mind! I'm not even sure I knew the definition of the word. How could you, *God*! I demanded an answer. My mother raised five sons and adopted another son and a daughter. Over many years, she accepted dozens of down-and-out foster children into our home. The Massachusetts Department of Social Services was routinely dropping off another kid. This is the thanks she gets? This is her end? How can it be? Why? How could you? From that day forward, and because of the questions I begged of God—more aptly, that I demanded of God—my life began to forge a new path. That old saying, "Be careful what you wish for," has some truth to it. The Bible says it more aptly: "Ask and you shall receive. Knock and the door shall be opened unto you." The answers to my angry, yet

DIVINE INTERVENTION

sincere, heartfelt questions began to arrive at diverse times and places and in diverse manners.

It was just a couple of months after my mom had passed away that Pam and I had to take our son Adam to the pediatrician. He was just under two and a half years old. Adam had a condition known as cough-variant asthma. At home, we had a nebulizer machine in order to treat his coughing flare-ups. In addition, he was often prescribed pediatric prednisone, an oral steroid to treat the inflammation of his airway, in addition to antibiotics. Dr. Peter Murphy was our pediatrician. He was always so kind and thoughtful; he was exceptional with our son. We so loved and immensely trusted Dr. Peter Murphy.

On this particular visit, we were waiting with our son for Dr. Murphy to enter the treatment room. Shortly thereafter, Dr. Murphy came into the room and greeted us. Immediately, Doc expressed his condolences regarding the passing of my mom. He made sure to tell me what a wonderful, beautiful person she was, and likewise, my dad too. He then turned his total attention to me. He shook my hand and looked directly into my eyes. I remember the soft, heartfelt expression in his eyes. Call me crazy, but I could feel his emotions and his whole demeanor reaching into the very depths of my heart. It was as if he was peering into my soul. He sensed and felt my sorrow. His compassion was heartwarming and appreciated. There was something in the whole exchange that got to me. He really touched my still-raw, grieving emotions. I wasn't quite sure how he knew my mom and dad and that Mom had passed away. I was thinking that he probably read her obituary recently. When I questioned him about that, Doc mentioned how he had met my parents previously in the office a couple months back. Mom and Dad had brought our son, Adam, in with an asthma flare-up. At that point, it all came back to my recollection. Pam and I were at a convention in Hawaii sponsored by the company I work for. While we were away, our little guy, Adam, had another cough-variant asthma flare-up. He was really sick and needed steroids, antibiotics, and nebulizer treatments again. Mom and Dad took Adam to see Dr. Murphy. She didn't tell us a blessed thing while we were in Hawaii. She wanted to spare us the worry.

After some time chatting with Dr. Murphy, somehow the conversation took an abrupt turn. I began to ask him about the two or three trips he took to other countries throughout the year. In fact, he had just gotten back from a trip to Indonesia. Dr. Murphy explained that he brought medicine and health care to the extremely poor indigenous people of those countries. I was blaming evil governments and their greed for allowing these circumstances to exist. My conversation was emphasizing the political and economic nature of their plight. He, on the other hand, was emphasizing the severe medical issues of these indigenous people and their overwhelming need to hear the gospel! *What!*

Dr. Murphy had a very kind and humble demeanor as he went on to explain his point. His

DIVINE INTERVENTION

emphasis was that, indeed, the evil of man's greed, hunger for power, and control were contributing factors to their abject poverty. In addition, he went on to say that these poor people needed to hear about Jesus Christ and the good news of salvation and eternal life. Through his dispensing of medical treatments and medicine, Doc would pour out his love and compassion for these folks. He truly wanted to make a difference in their lives. He would also tell them that there is a God and that God loves them. I was beginning to wonder how we transitioned from economics, governments, and politics to the person of Jesus Christ.

As we exited the treatment room and made our way into the main part of the office, *not* coincidentally, everyone had gone home. We were the last appointment of the day, and the entire staff was gone. Not a secretary or nurse had remained. My wife, our son, Dr. Murphy, and I were the only ones still in the office. At that point, our beloved pediatrician turned his entire focus on me. He began to expound further on the person of Jesus of Nazareth. I was open-minded and interested in his discourse. Doc was most definitely making an impact on me, or, should I say, the Holy Spirit was!

I will never forget the illustration, literally, that he used that late afternoon. He actually pulled out a prescription pad from his shirt pocket and began to draw something. It was eerily quiet for a second as he began to sketch. When Doc was done, he presented a crude stick figure drawing. A physician was he, certainly not an artist! The sketch illustrated a person stuck down in a hole with a sad face. Above the hole was another figure on flat ground, looking down while the person in the hole looked up. He explained how we were the figure stuck in the pit, weighted down by our sin nature and all the trials and tribulations of this life.

He went on to explain how every religious figure known throughout history comes to the side of that hole and offers you a way out of your plight. The remedy they proclaim is that you've got to do something! They suggest you give a certain percentage of your income every year or pray facing a specific geographical location three times a day, go to church, be a good person, perform certain rituals and sacraments, and on and on it goes. Even better, they say, it is imperative that you do lots of good work throughout your entire life. Perhaps help old folks cross the street, work in soup kitchens, build shelters for the homeless, and, most assuredly, don't kick any stray cats! I jest! All of these efforts, which these religious men spoke of, would elevate you up and out of the pit you're imprisoned in. Moreover, they claimed you'd be more enlightened.

Dr. Murphy also made it a point to remind me that all of these worldly sages offering this plethora of advice were still in their graves or tombs; their bodies are still there. Dr. Murphy continued, "True biblical Christianity" is where a man, Jesus, who, by the way, is alive and His tomb is empty. He comes to the side of the hole and sees you struggling in your plight of

DIVINE INTERVENTION

captivity. He then removes his cloak and sets it aside, then jumps down into the pit, puts you on his back, and carries you out. All you have to do is realize you are helpless to get out on your own. He extends this invitation freely, out of grace and love. To be rescued, you must simply trust and allow Him to rescue you. Trust Him wholly, who is holy, to make you whole. Simply allow Jesus to save you. He will voluntarily come down in the pit, and He alone will take on the burden and accomplish the task of restoring you to level ground. Indeed, He will be your Savior if you will allow Him to be.

As Dr. Murphy was explaining and illustrating this concept to me, my emotions began to rise. My eyes were beginning to fill, my chin started a tiny quiver, and the hair on the back of my head was rising and tingling. I felt as though I were being warmed from the inside out. All I could think of in that moment was *wow!* These are the words I've been waiting to hear all my life. They rang so clear and so true to me! What came to mind was that this sounds so easy! Dr. Murphy sensed my condition; it was written all over my face. He asked me if I wanted to know personally how to get out of that hole. I will never forget the sincerity and humility in his eyes as he quietly waited for my response. He did not pressure me in any way but looked upon me with love and compassion. I responded that I was in the process of doing some reading on my own at home and searching for some answers. It was the typical brush-off. I thanked him most sincerely for what he had expounded to me and for also taking such good care of our son. With that said, we bid our goodbyes and departed the office.

That day in Dr. Murphy's office began a journey for me. I was deeply touched by Dr. Murphy's concern for me and his willingness to share such a profound truth. With tremendous zeal and dedication, over the next five months, I read the entire New Testament. I read from the Gospel of Matthew straight through the book of Revelation. I was like a kid in a candy store! I stopped at nothing to pour over the Scriptures, not missing a period or an apostrophe along the way. Night after night and month after month, I read! I never, in my entire life, read such perfect, unadulterated truth! The words on the page made perfect sense; they seemed to come alive and jump off the page! My wife would come down from the bedroom at three o'clock in the morning only to find me with a pencil in my ear, an open notebook, a pen in my mouth, and a highlighter in hand. I was absolutely consumed with intrigue and wide-eyed wonder by what this book, the Bible, was detailing to me! In fact, the message seemed to be diametrically opposed to the religion I was taught throughout my youth. The words I read appeared to pull me away from religiosity and direct me more toward a person, Jesus of Nazareth.

Between the time when we visited Dr. Murphy and my entire reading of the New Testament, interestingly enough, some surprise visitors came knocking on my front door. Over the years, Jehovah's

DIVINE INTERVENTION

Witnesses came on occasion. I never considered them to have any truth or validity. However, this time, for the first time ever, the Mormons showed up! I graciously allowed two young men into my home. An Elder Jones and an Elder Smith, as it were. I've disguised their real names to protect the innocent—again, I jest! What immediately became apparent was that I had two eighteen-year-old kids, fifteen years my junior, with the prefix Elder. These young kids were attempting to tell me about life and death. They brought out the Bible from their briefcase and set it on my coffee table for a brief moment. They never really discussed its contents in any depth. Very soon after, however, they brought their book out. It was entitled *The Book of Mormon: Another Testament of Jesus Christ*.

Their sales pitch actually sounded somewhat interesting; it was beginning to appeal to my intellect. After about an hour of listening to a completely strange, different dialogue and theology than what I had been reading in the Bible, I had had enough! I sent away the two "Elder" youngins, clad in their white shirts, black ties, and name tag placards. That evening, I called Dr. Murphy at his home phone number, which he had given me. I reiterated to him the CliffsNotes of my conversation with the "Elder" Mormons and their crazy doctrine. I wanted to know his take on that sect's beliefs. He first insisted that I stop calling him Dr. Murphy and suggested I call him Pete. Secondly, he asked me if we'd known each other long enough that he could be frank with me. My response was, of course! He then went on to explain to me, with much zeal, I might add, "Mormon theology was scribed in the pits of hell in order to distract human beings from the simplicity of the Gospel of Jesus Christ!" To which I commented on how harsh that condemnation was. At that moment, he invited Pam and me to a cookout at his house that Saturday afternoon.

Later on, after the meal, he conducted a little Bible study and a question-and-answer time, followed by a time of prayer. It was all very novel to me, yet at the same time, I felt my heartstrings being tugged on. When I left, I was handed a Bible tract detailing how to become a Christian. I went home and continued my reading quest of the New Testament.

It was nearly six months since watching my mom pass away in February 1992, and about five months after my encounter with Dr. Murphy in his office. Around the third week of August 1992, I was in my living room and had completely finished reading the entire New Testament. I pulled out that Bible tract given to me at the cookout and read through it thoroughly. The tract spells out how a person can become a Christian. It was encapsulated by words and pictures—everything the Bible had taught me over those last six months.

God had divinely intervened in my life those past six months, in the same way as He did my entire life, as evidenced in the previous chapters of this book. God ultimately delivered me to that precise moment in my living room around eleven thirty in the evening. I was alone. Well, I wasn't really alone; God was with me. Pam and my two-and-a-half-year-old son Adam were asleep. I closed the Bible, I set down the Bible tract, and I closed my eyes. I prayed to God and thanked Him for bringing me on this journey and opening my eyes and my heart to the truth—the truth I discovered in His Word, the Bible. I had so much to tell Him in my prayer. With tears in my eyes, I spoke of how I had believed in God and Jesus all of my life up to that point. I literally even said that if someone had just broken into my house and demanded that I renounce that there is a God and that Jesus is His only Son, I would not comply! I would refuse. I insisted, even if they threatened me with death or the death of my sleeping family! I reiterated with extreme fervor that I would not renounce Him! I would *not* renounce Him! I continued praying that I now realized something was missing in my life.

After reading God's word for six months that August night, I humbly admitted to God my need for a Savior. Please, Jesus, I prayed. Will you have what you did on the cross be appropriated to my sin? I have taken my personal inventory and realize that, in thought, word, and deed, I have sinned against you time and time again throughout my entire life. It seems to come so easy and so natural. I'm so sorry, Father God. Please forgive me! Jesus, I pray that You please, with Your righteous shed blood, cleanse me from all my sins—my sins of yesterday and today— and every sin I will commit till the day I die! Please come into my heart and into my life. Save me, Lord Jesus, and be my Savior. Thank You for forgiving me, saving my soul, and giving me an eternal life in Your presence in Your kingdom! Thank You for taking my sin and the punishment for it upon Your body on the cross. I am so sorry You had to endure that for me! Thank You for being patient with me all these years and for loving and protecting me since my birth. Thank You for watching over me and for not giving up on me. You watched over me and divinely intervened many times and with perfect timing. You wove through my life like a beautiful tapestry. You were always there—the thread that held me together. You persevered after me and preserved my life so that this very night would arrive. This You have done so graciously in order that Your plan for my life would come to fruition. Thank You, God; thank You, Jesus; and thank You, Holy Spirit, for all Your divine interventions throughout my life. It would appear that You have ordered my life's footsteps. To You, Lord, be all praise, glory, and honor. Great things You have done! I love You, God! Now, Lord, please, I pray in Jesus's name. Please help me to live a life worthy of the calling to which You have called me to evangelize the lost.

Since that August night in 1992 in the quiet of my living room, I have never been the same. God changed me from the inside out. I was once blind, but now I see. My sin no longer hangs over me like a thousand-pound weight. My guilt for the bad things I've done and for the things I know I should have

DIVINE INTERVENTION

done but didn't has all but disappeared. I've been made a new creation in Christ. The old Joe has been mortified. The new Joe has been spiritually reborn and lives day by day through the grace and mercy of God. I was physically born in May of 1962. My mother delivered me from her body at Somerville Hospital in Somerville, Massachusetts. That is a matter of historical record, as testified to by a birth certificate at Somerville City Hall. In August of 1992, almost thirty years later to the date, I was "born again" spiritually in the quiet of my living room.

This supernatural event happened when I realized I was a sinner, repented of my sin, and trusted that Jesus's blood sacrifice and broken body on the cross were for the remission and forgiveness of my sin. He paid it all! Jesus secured my pardon and reconciliation; He paid the ransom! He took the penalty for my sins and bore the punishment on the cross that should have been mine. The incredible result of his sacrifice is that I'm forgiven! I was a captive down in the hole, and now I've been set free—rescued! There is a mansion in heaven awaiting my arrival. I did not earn it, nor do I deserve it. It is a gift from God's grace, laid aside for me and coupled with eternal life in a new and glorified, incorruptible body. No human words can express my level of gratitude to my God, my Creator, and my Savior, who love me so much. He continuously and divinely intervened in my life over so many years in order that I might be *saved*! As the hymn says, "Praise Him, praise Him, Jesus, our blessed Redeemer!"

The Gospel

The *gospel*. We sometimes hear that word thrown about in various secular phrases and clichés. For example, I was home all night; I swear, that's the gospel truth! Or what he just said is pure gospel! Just one more example: you can't take everything she says as gospel truth. Outside of its application to religion, the word gospel is also used to describe an idea or rule that's accepted as undoubtedly true. From a religious or biblical viewpoint, the word *gospel* is derived from the Koine Greek language, or common Greek. It is a dead language today. However, ancient Greek is richer, more complex, and more precise than modern languages. It was the ancient language of Alexander the Great. Literally interpreted, it means good news! I think that it's no coincidence that the New Testament was originally written in Koine Greek. I believe our Creator and God wanted the message of salvation spelled out in a precise language where one word meant one thing. In this regard, there would be no room for confusion, misinterpretation, or doubt as to the meaning and His design for the human

DIVINE INTERVENTION

race. God wanted His creation to have a correct and truthful understanding of His plan of redemption for our eternal souls. I guess, in legal terms, you could call it full disclosure. As a result, mankind would be fully informed and, hence, would be, without excuse, unable to claim ignorance, on judgment day!

Oftentimes, we hear the phrase, "Would you like to hear the good news first or the bad news?" I think hearing the bad news first helps us to better appreciate when we hear the good news as a follow-up. According to the Bible, the bad news is that mankind is inherently flawed. The Bible calls this flaw sin and proclaims that everyone ever born has this congenital birth defect, except for Jesus. He was not born via conventional means through the seed of Joseph, or else he would be flawed just like the rest of humanity. Instead, Jesus was conceived by the Holy Spirit through a virgin birth. Hence, Joseph's sin nature was not passed along to Him through intercourse with Mary. Jesus was without sin, and He never sinned throughout the entire thirty-three years of His life. This is supernatural! Get used to that fact, because the Bible is a supernatural book full of the supernatural workings of God.

The bad news continues: The Apostle Paul in the book of Romans proclaims, "There is none righteous, no not one" (Rom. 3:10). Additionally, Paul says, "For all have sinned and come short of the glory of God" (Rom. 3:23). He says, "Wherefore, as by one man, (Adam), sin entered into the world, and death by sin; so death passed upon all men, for that all have sinned" (Rom. 5:12). Then he puts the hammer down as he heralds, "For the wages of sin is death, but the gift of God is eternal life through Jesus Christ our Lord" (Rom. 6:23). That last proclamation of scripture by the apostle Paul contains both the bad news first and then, after the conjunction word *but*, the good news (gospel), as a follow-up. There is no getting around it. We are all sinners naturally, from birth. The things we want to do and know we should do, we don't do. The things we know we shouldn't do and don't want to do, we do. It comes naturally. The prophet Isaiah said it best: "All we like sheep have gone astray; we have turned everyone to his own way" (Isa. 53:6). As a result of this inherent sin nature, the Apostle Paul proclaims, We all die! We've all been handed a death sentence! Death is imminent!

In the garden of Eden, our Creator made perfectly known to our first human parents the consequence of disobedience: "And the LORD God commanded the man saying, of every tree of the garden thou mayest freely eat: But of the tree of the knowledge of good and evil, thou shalt not eat of it: for in that day that thou eatest thereof, thou shalt surely die" (Gen. 2:16–17). This death is both physical and spiritual. Physically, our temporal, mortal bodies will die one day and then decay in the earth: "In the sweat of thy face shalt thy eat bread, till thou return unto the ground; for out of it wast thou taken: for dust thou art, and unto dust shalt thou return" (Gen. 2:16–17). From the spiritual perspective, our eternal soul and spirit will be separated from our phys-

DIVINE INTERVENTION

ical bodies and stand in the judgment: "And as it is appointed unto men once to die but after this the judgment" (Heb. 9:27). So much for reincarnation and the caste system—the false notion that you die and keep coming back until you achieve perfection, a.k.a. Nirvana. There will be no coming back; there will be no do-overs until you get it right.

Outside of a saving faith in Christ, there will be death and judgment—period! There will be no fellowship with God, no relationship with our Creator, no heaven, no streets of gold or crystal sea, and no rest for your soul. *Ugh!* In fact, we will be consigned to a place originally prepared for the devil, Lucifer, and the fallen angels, a.k.a. demons! This is a fearful, godforsaken place defined by eternal suffering and torment. It is called hell: "And the smoke of their torment ascendeth up for ever and ever and they have no rest day or night" (Rev. 14:11). As crazy as it may sound, it should be noted that Jesus spoke about hell ten times more often than He did about heaven. I would suggest that clearly, He was warning us. By the way, the word *satan*, literally translated from the Koine Greek, means your enemy or adversary. As mentioned, hell was originally designed for the devil and his angels. Since man inherited the sin nature and is now a fallen being, man, like Satan, is under condemnation. Because all humanity has sinned against God, the Bible says, Hell has been expanded: "Therefore Hell hath enlarged herself and opened her mouth without measure" (Isa. 5:14). Make no mistake about it: the devil, Satan, our enemy and adversary, wants our eternal destiny to reside with him and his fallen angels in his godforsaken abode!

From the beginning, in the garden of Eden, his diabolical design was to corrupt our first human parents and lead them away from God, their heavenly Father and Creator. This was the fall of humanity, with cataclysmic eternal consequences! Satan wanted to and continues to rob humanity of its rightful inheritance. Satan's evil and diabolical plan of destruction in the garden incorporated confusion, deceit, pride, fear, and doubt in order to convince Adam and Eve of his lies and undermine God's word, His truth, and His authority. Satan's ultimate goal was to bring them under condemnation by disobeying God's commands. If Satan could accomplish that, then God, true to His word, would have to bring death as judgment on mankind, as He had openly declared. Satan was successful in convincing Adam and Eve that his way was superior to God's way: "And the serpent said unto the woman, Ye shall surely not die: for God doth know that in the day ye eat thereof, then your eyes shall be opened, and ye shall be as gods, knowing good and evil" (Gen. 3:4–6). Our original parents harkened to Satan's lies and condemned all humanity to inherit the sin curse and to die a temporal physical death. Yet even worse is to die an eternal spiritual death, which would separate us from our Creator for all eternity. Just look how that turned out! We inherited a nature that is sinful, corrupted, and against the righteous nature and will of our Creator. "The apple doesn't fall far from

DIVINE INTERVENTION

the tree." We naturally tend to live more like and for the devil than we do for our God and Creator. As a drastic result, the address of our postmortem eternal estate and destiny has been changed!

We can correctly glean from the previously noted verses of scripture that, indeed, all of humanity has a serious problem. Because the wage of sin is *death,* then we truly have a problem of biblical proportions! Surely, our God and Creator would not leave us in this state of condemnation. If this were to be the eventuality of all mankind, what hope would there be for us? What joy could we possess? What would be the reason for living? Is not our God a God of love and mercy? Weren't we designed to have eternal fellowship with our Creator? There has to be more to the story! Surely, God has a plan to solve humanity's sin curse problem and rescue us from the consequences thereof. Yes, indeed! Our loving and merciful God has a plan of restoration and redemption! He has a plan for forgiveness and reconciliation—a plan of grace and mercy; a plan of atonement and justification; a plan to bring us into His kingdom; a plan to restore us to our original rightful inheritance in beautiful and perfect fellowship with the Father, Son, and Holy Spirit. His plan is to transform us into eternal, incorruptible, and immortal sons and daughters of the most high God! He will blot out our sins and remember them no more. His plan covers us in righteousness and allows us to call Him *Abba,* which literally, interpreted from the Koine Greek, means daddy.

God has accomplished his divine plan and remedied our sin nature. The cure for man's sin problem lies in the second half of the verse of scripture noted above: "For the wages of sin is death; BUT the GIFT of God is eternal life through Jesus Christ Our Lord." Did you catch those key words: *but, gift, eternal life, through,* and *Jesus Christ our Lord?*

I love to receive gifts! Who doesn't? Do you remember when our earthly parents bought us birthday gifts? It was awesome! They gave them to us to celebrate the day we were born because they loved us and wanted us to be happy. How much better would it be to receive a gift of eternal duration from God Himself, from our heavenly parents, the Father, Son, and Holy Spirit! That is exactly what God has done for each and every one of us who reside here on planet earth. We've been given the gift of eternal life. There are enumerable verses of scripture that illustrate what God has done out of His pure love for us. His gift to mankind is far more precious than silver or gold. I'll share just a handful of Bible verses, but in no way exhaust the totality of the list. The bad news we got first was really, really bad! However, now let's take a look at the "good news."

The good news is exceptionally good news! We've been given a gift by God of eternal life through Jesus Christ, our Lord. Carefully consider the verses of scripture below. I offer no commentary on them. I trust the Holy Spirit will give your heart and mind what is necessary in order to decipher the truth and its profound meaning. Ponder them and consider

DIVINE INTERVENTION

them as if your eternal life depends on them, because it does!

Jesus said, "For God so loved the world that he gave his only begotten Son, that whosoever believeth in him should not perish, but have everlasting life" (John 3:16).

> For God sent not his Son into the world to condemn the world; but that the world through Him might be saved. (John 3:17)

> He that believeth on him is not condemned: but he that believeth not is condemned already, because he hath not believed in the name of the only begotten Son of God. (John 3:18)

> But God commendeth his love to us, in that while we were yet sinners, Christ died for us. Much more then, being now justified by his blood, we shall be saved from wrath through him. (Rom 5:8–9)

> Jesus said unto her, I am the resurrection, and the life: he that believeth in me, though he were dead, yet shall he live. And who-

soever lives and believes in me shall never die. (John 11:25–26)

That God was in Christ reconciling the world unto himself, not counting people's sins against them. And he has committed to us the message of reconciliation. (2 Cor. 5:19)

God made him, (Jesus), who had no sin to be sin for us, so that in him we might become the righteousness of God. (2 Cor. 5:21)

Therefore, there is now no more condemnation to them that are in Christ Jesus. (Rom. 8:1)

Who his own self bare our sins in his own body on a tree, that we, being dead to sins, should live unto righteousness: by whose stripes ye are healed. (1 Pet. 2:24)

For Christ also hath once suffered for sins, the just for the unjust, that he might bring us to God, being put to death in

DIVINE INTERVENTION

> the flesh, but quickened, (made
> alive), by the Spirit. (1 Pet. 3:18)

I could literally go on for days with pages and pages of scripture verses in reference to Jesus's sacrificial death and atonement, His resurrection, and Him being the Savior of the world. In Matthew's gospel, Jesus states, "Even as the Son of man came not to be ministered unto, but to minister and give his life a ransom for many" (Matt. 20:28). Again, in the Gospel of John, we read where Jesus says, "I am the way, the truth and the life, no man cometh unto the Father but by me" (John 14:6).

It could not be any clearer that the consequence of man's sin is death, both physical and spiritual, but God has given us a way out. He has commuted our death sentence and punished Jesus in our place. The judge of all the universe did not just abandon justice and sweep the penalty for sin under the carpet. It was decided in eternity past, before the earth was even spinning in space, that Jesus the Son would volunteer and come down to earth. The Creator putting on the created! He would sacrifice His life on a cross so that we could go free. Our sin would not be held to our charge; the slate would be wiped clean; and the sin debt would be paid in full! He bore the punishment that we deserved. Jesus said, "I lay down my life, that I might take it again. No man takes it from me but I lay it down of myself" (John 10:17–18). Jesus is our substitute, our Redeemer, and our Savior. A supernatural exchange took place on the cross. Our filthy sin was placed on Jesus, and His perfect righteousness was draped over us like a cloak.

So now, when the Father looks at us, He doesn't see sin; He sees Jesus! Jesus has placed us under his protective wing: "The blood of Jesus Christ his son cleanses us from all sin" (1 Jn 1:7). Jesus's righteousness was imputed (attributed) to us. Despite who we are or were, along with the heinous sins we have committed against God, we now appear holy and righteous and without blemish before God: "And, having made peace through the blood of his cross, by him to reconcile all things unto himself, I say whether they be things in earth, or heaven" (Col. 1:20). Simply amazing, beyond compare! Praise God!

Conclusion

What conclusions have you come to? Who do you consider this person, Jesus of Nazareth, to be? Most people believe in Jesus; you would be silly not to. He is mentioned in the *Encyclopedia Britannica*, a secular book, as a religious leader revered in Christianity. When it comes right down to it, it doesn't take faith to believe in Jesus of Nazareth. He was a bona fide person who lived in the past. That is an irrefutable fact. He is a part of the historical record, even outside of the biblical text. His magnificent teachings on life and God are still with us today. He gave us the golden rule. Our calendars bear silent witness to Him in BC and AD. You can travel to where He was born, ministered, crucified, laid in a tomb, and rose again. All these facts are indisputable. Who you believe Jesus really was is where the rubber meets the road. It is a matter of believing *on* Jesus. The Bible says, "Thou believeth that there is one God; thou doest well. The devils also believe and tremble" (James 2:19). It may sound like petty semantics; however, it's the difference between heaven and hell! There is a vast difference between believing *in* Jesus and believing *on* Jesus. Again, the devil and the demons believe in Jesus. The demons even spoke with Jesus through possessed men. They clearly knew Jesus from eternity past. However, they don't get a second chance to repent. Maybe it is because they were there in heaven with God and knew better, yet still rebelled against God. They had tasted of the splendor, glory, and majesty of God. They would never repent anyway! We humans, however, get a second chance to call upon God and ask forgiveness.

Was Jesus of Nazareth a mere man or prophet, or was he the God-man—God incarnate, taking care of humanity's penalty for sin on a cruel and torturous Roman cross? Do you believe and trust that He was crucified, buried, and ultimately, on the third day, rose from the dead? Your answer to that question will determine your eternal fate and final destination. I for one believe that "God became flesh and dwelt among us and we beheld His glory, the glory, as of the only begotten of the Father full of grace and truth" (John 1:14).

God has given man free will. Countless Bible verses make it abundantly clear that man has an opportunity, a choice, to accept Jesus's free gift of salvation: "Choose you this day whom you will serve, as for me and my house, we will serve the LORD" (Josh. 24:15). Salvation is a free gift to us and costs us nothing; however, it cost Jesus everything; He paid the full measure. He extends His hand down

DIVINE INTERVENTION

from the cross and invites you to grab on, take hold, and accept His offer of forgiveness and reconciliation. This is a gift of tremendous magnitude and eternal value! Jesus's blood cleanses us from all our guilty stains. Jesus says, "Come onto me, all ye that labor and are heavy-laden, I will give you rest" (Matt. 11:28). Additionally, He proclaims, "Behold I stand at the door and knock: if any man hear my voice, and open the door, I will come in to him, and will sup with him, and he with me" (Rev. 3:20).

It's not enough to have factual head knowledge of who Jesus is. It's not enough to think you are religious or spiritual. It's not enough, so say you've completed and accomplished thus and so within a certain denomination. It's not enough to think you are good enough, have merited favor by your good works, and deserve to reside in heaven. Salvation isn't about sacraments, rituals, creeds, heritage, traditions, denominations, or church membership. The Apostle Paul declares, "For by grace are you saved through faith; and not that of yourselves: it is the gift of God: not of your own works, lest any man should boast" (Eph. 2:8–9). By its very nature, salvation is a gift, and a gift isn't earned. A gift is given, bestowed freely out of love. Scripture tells us, better yet, warns us to call out to Him and ask for forgiveness and to repent of our sins. To repent simply means to take an inventory of yourself and recognize that you, indeed, are a sinner, guilty as charged. It means that upon this realization, you turn one hundred and eighty degrees away from the idea that you can save yourself. If you didn't need saving, then Jesus would never have had to come down: "This is a faithful saying, and worthy of all acceptance, that Christ Jesus came into the world to save sinners, of whom I am chief" (1 Tim. 1:15).

The simple fact is that only through what Jesus did for us on the cross, through his bodily sacrifice and shed blood, do we inherit eternal life and the kingdom of God. Again, it is His gift to us. Jesus said, "I tell you, nay: but except ye repent ye shall all likewise perish" (Luke 3:5). Again, there are dozens of Scripture verses that reference this fact. There are too many to fit in this little book. Just a few more scripture verses to drive home the point of how to be saved and know with certainty that heaven will be your home and Jesus is your personal Savior. The Apostle Paul emphatically states, "That if thou shalt confess with thy mouth the Lord Jesus, and shalt believe in thy heart that God raised him from the dead, thou shalt be saved. For with the heart man believeth unto righteousness; and with the mouth confession is made unto salvation. For the scripture saith, whosoever believeth on him shall not be ashamed. For there is no difference between the Jew and the Greek: for the same Lord over all is rich unto all that call upon him. For whosoever shall call upon the name of the LORD shall be saved" (Rom. 9:9–13). Jesus said, "Whosoever therefore shall confess me before men, him will I confess also before my Father which is in Heaven. But whosoever shall deny me before men, him will I also deny before my Father which is in heaven" (Matt. 10:32–33).

DIVINE INTERVENTION

The great author of the book of Acts was Luke, a noted first-century historian and physician. His writings comprise most of the New Testament, along with the Gospel of Luke and the book of Acts. He had this to say about Jesus: "Neither is there salvation in any other: for there is none other name under heaven given among men whereby we must be saved" (Acts 4:12). When the Apostle Paul wrote to the Philippian church, he said, "That at the name of Jesus every knee should bow, of things in heaven, and things in earth, and things under the earth; and that every tongue should confess that Jesus Christ is Lord, to the glory of God the Father" (Phil. 2:10–11). "How shall we escape, if we neglect so great salvation; which at the first began to be spoken by the Lord and was confirmed unto us by them that heard Him" (Heb. 2:3).

Invitation

I sincerely hope and pray that these personal events I've shared with you about my life have in some way triggered some emotions and questions about your own life. I wonder if you can recognize the times and circumstances when God was actively, divinely intervening and weaving his way through the tapestry of your life. Is it possible that you've read this book because God has ordered your footsteps and you are right where you're supposed to be? Perhaps there are many similar events and situations that you've experienced from your youth until the present day. Life is so hectic and busy that it becomes cluttered with so many distractions. Often, these distractions can keep us from seeing God's miraculous, perfectly timed workings in our own lives, literally right before our very eyes. All along, He has been watching, protecting, and wooing you. You may not have been looking for Him, but He was always keeping an eye on you. On the other hand, maybe you've written some of these life events off to happenstance, mere coincidence, or luck. My prayer for you is that this book has awakened a heartfelt zeal

173

to reconsider where and when God has divinely intervened in the timeline of your life. Perhaps this book has stirred you to realize that many times you have been lovingly nudged, supernaturally protected, and miraculously sought after by your heavenly Father. Perhaps this book in and of itself is a glaring sign in your life's journey toward salvation and knowing Jesus personally.

> The Lord is not slack concerning his promise, as some men count slackness; but he is long-suffering to usward, not willing that any should perish but that all should come to repentance. (2 Pet. 3:9)

> "As I live, sayeth the Lord GOD, I have no pleasure in the death of the wicked. (Ezek. 33:11)

Contrarily, the Bible says, "Precious in the sight of the LORD is the death of his saints (believers)" (Proverbs 116:15). When we come home to Him, it is a precious moment. I think that's because God can't wait to see us and give us that immortal, incorruptible, new spiritual body along with all that heaven has to offer! God is patient beyond compare. He loves you and desires fellowship with you for all eternity in heaven.

Jesus stands at the door and knocks. He is patiently and lovingly waiting for you to open the

DIVINE INTERVENTION

door of your heart and ask Him in to receive His forgiveness. Jesus has already paid the price; now He awaits your response to His gift. No one is promised another day. Will you call on Him while you are able? While there still remains breath in your lungs? Don't delay; don't put off for tomorrow what you can do today! Even now, today is the accepted hour of your salvation. Your words to Him need not be eloquent, articulate, or even long-winded. Jesus will know what you are asking for because He knows your heart and the deepest thoughts and intents therein. He will know exactly why it is that you've come to Him. Surrender your life to the Savior. Let Him know that you're aware that, indeed, you are a sinner, needy of His forgiveness. The angels in heaven are awaiting to celebrate your salvation, as your name will be written down in the Lamb's Book of Life. I am certain that when we die, we will meet Jesus. I am also certain, according to God's Word, that we will hear either one proclamation or another from Him. One being, "Well done thou good and faithful servant enter into the joy of the Lord" (Matt. 25:23). The other being, "And then I will declare to them, I never knew you; depart from me, you workers of lawlessness" (Matt. 7:23). If you're relying on His broken body and shed blood alone, apart from anything else, then in no way does it have to be the later proclamation you'll hear!

> Whosoever shall call upon the name of the Lord shall be saved. (Rom. 10:13)

Won't you RSVP today? Plan to attend the heavenly ceremony known as the marriage supper of the Lamb. Reach up with a hand and heart of faith and reserve your presence in glory by accepting Jesus's sacrifice. Ask Him to appropriate what He did on the cross for you. That's what I said in August of 1992! Your admission price is paid in full! He is waiting for you to call: "But as many as received him, (Jesus), to them gave he power to become the sons of God even to them that believe on his name" (John 1:12). Receive Him today! All praise, honor, and glory be given unto the Lamb of God who taketh away the sins of the world, the King of kings and Lord of lords. Thank You, Jesus, for saving our souls!

About the Author

Joe Cappucci resides in West Townsend, Massachusetts, with his wife, Pamela. They have four grown children: Adam, Christian, Anthony, and Olivia. He attended North Adams State College in the Berkshires of North Western Massachusetts, later graduating from Fitchburg State college in 1985 in Fitchburg, Massachusetts. He received a bachelor of science in business management with a minor in Spanish. He speaks Spanish fluently and enjoys engaging in Spanish conversations when encountering Latinos. Going to the gym to work out and sitting on a beach at the ocean in Maine or New Hampshire are his favorite pastimes. His overwhelming desire is to share true biblical Christianity, the gospel, with everyone he meets, if not in word then by deed. Full-time evangelism is the heartbeat of his life: "I just want to tell people about what Jesus did for us."

www.ingramcontent.com/pod-product-compliance
Lightning Source LLC
Chambersburg PA
CBHW030748290125
20903CB00067B/602